The Ivy Portfolio

How to Invest Like the Top Endowments and Avoid Bear Markets

Mebane T. Faber
Eric W. Richardson

WILEY

John Wiley & Sons, Inc.

Published by John Wiley & Sons, Inc., Hoboken, New Jersey.
Published simultaneously in Canada.

For general information on our other products and services or for technical support, please contact our Customer Care Department within the United States at (800) 762-2974, outside the United States at (317) 572-3993 or fax (317) 572-4002.

Wiley also publishes its books in a variety of electronic formats. Some content that appears in print may not be available in electronic books. For more information about Wiley products, visit our web site at www.wiley.com.

Library of Congress Cataloging-in-Publication Data
Faber, Mebane T., 1977-
    The ivy portfolio: how to invest like the top endowments and avoid bear markets
Mebane T. Faber, Eric W. Richardson.
        p.   cm.
Includes bibliographical references and Index.
ISBN 978-1-118-00885-0 (paper)

    1. Portfolio management.   2. Investments.   3.   Institutional investments.
    I. Richardson, Eric W., 1966-   II. Title.
HG4529.5.F333   2009
332.6—dc22
                                                                2008034565

10 9 8 7 6 5 4 3 2 1

To Gama and Boondock

To my parents, Larry and Marilyn Richardson

*A portion of all book proceeds will go to
local animal rescue shelters.*

Contents

Preface   ix
Acknowledgments   xi

Part One: Constructing Your Ivy Portfolio   1

Chapter 1   The Super Endowments   3
             Endowments Are Different   4
             Size Matters . . .   8
             . . . and So Does Performance   11
             Active Management over Passive   14
             Summary   16
Chapter 2   The Yale Endowment   17
             History of the Endowment   18
             David Swensen's Ascent   22
             Of Alphas and Betas   30
             Outlining the Yale Process   33
             Domestic Equity   34
             Foreign Equity   35
             Fixed-Income   37
             Real Assets   37
             Private Equity   38
             Summary   39
Chapter 3   The Harvard Endowment   41
             History of the Endowment   42
             The Owner's Mentality   43

	Harvard's Swensen	45
	More Money, More Problems	48
	How Harvard Does It	50
	Summary	53
Chapter 4	Building Your Own Ivy League Portfolio	55
	Do as I Do—Shadowing the Super Endowments	56
	Risk-Adjusted Returns	64
	Do as I Say	66
	Inflation Is the Enemy	68
	Creating an All-Weather Policy Portfolio through Indexing	71
	Implementing Your Portfolio	74
	Rebalancing Your Portfolio	77
	Summary	78
	Part Two: Alternatives	**81**
Chapter 5	Private Equity	83
	What Is Private Equity?	84
	Historical Returns and Benchmarking	85
	How to Invest in Publicly Listed Private Equity	91
	Summary	96
Chapter 6	Hedge Funds	97
	A Brief Introduction to Hedge Funds	98
	Fund of Funds	101
	Options to Invest in Hedge Funds	113
	Individual Hedge Funds	123
	Fund of Funds	125
	Practical Considerations	131
	Summary	132
	Part Three: Active Management	**133**
Chapter 7	Winning by Not Losing	135
	Losing Hurts	136
	The Quantitative System	141
	Out-of-Sample Testing and Systematic Tactical Asset Allocation	151

	Extensions	158
	A Rotation System	159
	Practical Considerations and Taxes	160
	Discipline	162
	The Systems versus the Endowments	165
	Why It Works	166
	Summary	169
Chapter 8	Following the Smart Money	171
	Introduction to the 13F	172
	Combining the Top Fund Managers to Create Your Own Fund of Funds	182
	Summary	185
Chapter 9	Develop an Action Plan	187
	Implementing Your Ivy Portfolio	188
	Portfolios Discussed in *The Ivy Portfolio*	191

Appendix A: A Brief Review of Momentum and Trend Following	195
Appendix B: Additional Charts	199
Appendix C: Recommended Reading	207
Bibliography	211
About the Authors	218
Index	219

Preface

What do I do?

Many investors are asking themselves this very question after virtually every asset class faced large losses in 2008. Stocks, real estate, commodities, and even many hedge funds saw their values decline by 30% or more. Faced with this difficult backdrop, investors are re-examining how they should be managing their investment portfolio. How can *The Ivy Portfolio* help to preserve an investors' nest egg in this environment?

This book begins by examining the theory, process, and discipline behind the success of the two largest endowments: Yale University and Harvard University. Aimed at the novice investor and seasoned professional alike, this book demystifies the techniques that the ivory tower academic practitioners use to manage their portfolios. With the endowment Policy Portfolios as a guide, *The Ivy Portfolio* shows an investor how to build a core asset allocation of diverse asset classes to generate stable returns in various economic environments.

Next, *The Ivy Portfolio* details a simple method of tactical asset allocation that would have shielded an investor's portfolio from the large declines in asset classes in 2008. Avoiding costly bear markets is essential to conserve the capital in a portfolio, and this method did an admirable job in 2008.

Lastly, the book details how to follow the smart money by piggy-backing on the top hedge funds and their stock picking capabilities to form a stock portfolio. A simple method of following Warren Buffett's stock picks has outperformed the S&P 500 by over 10% a year since 1976. An investor can then go on to form a diversified fund of funds of the top managers, all the while retaining the ability to manage the individual holdings.

A question the reader might ask: "With dozens of asset allocation books on the market, and two books by one of the best portfolio managers of all time, why in the world do we need another book on the subject?" This book is not another primer on asset allocation. In fact, we recommend one of the great books by Roger Gibson (*Asset Allocation*) or David Darst (*Mastering the Art of Asset Allocation*) as a good prerequisite read to this book for those unfamiliar with the field of asset allocation.

Investors interested in the writings of the master himself can read David Swensen's books geared toward the professional investor—*Pioneering Portfolio Management*—and the individual investor—*Unconventional Success*. Likewise, there are many better primers on hedge funds, private equity, and the endowments (you can review the Reading List in this book for examples).

The intention behind *The Ivy Portfolio* is to deliver a highly readable book that profiles the top endowments and then examines how an investor can hope to replicate their returns while avoiding bear markets. The focus will be on practical applications that an investor can implement immediately to take control of their investment portfolio.

Throughout the book numerous papers and topics will be mentioned that are not in the scope of the book. The web site for the book, www.theivyportfolio.com, will provide links to some of the white papers and other source material discussed in this book. We welcome comments and questions, and readers can e-mail the authors at ivy@ cambriainvestments.com with feedback.

Acknowledgments

What started as an afternoon trying to find out the best way to hedge a long-only portfolio ended up first as a research paper, then as a blog, then an entire book. There have been numerous people and organizations that have helped us along the way.

We would first like to thank Larry Winer and Daniel Sanborn at Ned Davis Research for all of the outstanding work they have done in creating the charts for the book. The work produced by Ned Davis Research is consistently the gold standard in the quantitative research business.

Thanks to all of the readers of our blog World Beta. Your e-mails, comments, and suggestions have opened up many more avenues for research than we could have ever imagined.

Thanks to Mazin Jadallah for having the entrepreneurial drive to take a blog post and turn it into a software company. We would also like to thank James Altucher for his insight and encouragement regarding the 13F research process, as well as Scott Hiltebrant for help in backtesting the original models by hand. Thanks to Professor Griffin for the introduction to the hedge fund world.

Thanks to Chris Clark, Wayne Faber, and Scott Banerjee for your help in editing the early manuscripts, and Lindsay Trout for the willingness to share. We would like to acknowledge Eric Crittenden and Cole Wilcox at Blackstar for allowing us to use their charts in this book.

Thanks to Jessica Shedd at NACUBO, Bryan Taylor at Global Financial Data, Cambridge Associates, the Hennessee Group, Credit Suisse/Tremont, and Hedge Fund Research for allowing us to use their data in this book.

We would also like to thank the editors and publishers at Wiley who put up with our constant requests and revisions. Laura, Bill, and Emilie, thank you.

Thanks to all of the pioneers at the top endowments, foundations, and investment funds—without all of your work, this book would have been impossible.

Most important of all, this book would not be possible without the support of our families and friends; thank you to every one of you.

Part One

CONSTRUCTING YOUR IVY PORTFOLIO

Chapter 1

The Super Endowments

16.62%.

T hat figure is the annualized return the Yale University endowment has returned per year between 1985 and 2008.[1] To put
that number into perspective, the S&P 500 Index returned
11.98% a year over the same time period in one of the greatest bull markets in U.S. history.

Not only did the Yale endowment outperform stocks by over 4%
per year, but it did so with 33% less volatility and only one losing year (a
measly −0.2% in 1988). Similarly, the Harvard University endowment
returned over 15% a year with less than 10% volatility.[2] When the S&P
500 declined by 30% from June 2000 to June 2003, the Yale endowment
gained roughly 20% and the Harvard endowment returned 9%.

A $100,000 investment in the Yale endowment in 1985 would be
worth $4.0 million by June 2008, versus only $1.5 million invested in
the S&P 500 and $950,000 in U.S. 10-year government bonds. The
same amount invested in the Harvard endowment would be worth a
respectable $3.0 million.

---

[1]The endowment fiscal year ends June 30th; therefore, the yearly returns for the
indexes will look slightly different from the calendar year ending December 31st.
[2]Volatility is measured as the standard deviation of yearly returns unless noted
otherwise.

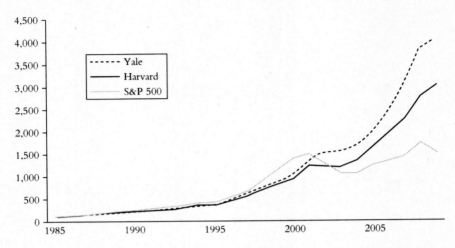

Figure 1.1   Equity Curve of the Yale and Harvard Endowments vs. the S&P 500, 1985–2008, Fiscal Year Ending June 30th
Source: Harvard and Yale endowment annual reports.

Figure 1.1 shows the performance of the top two endowments (by size) versus the S&P 500.

How exactly did Yale and Harvard accomplish such great returns, and more important, can an individual investor hope to achieve similar success? That is the focus of this book—a glimpse into the ivory tower to combine the best of academia and the real world to manage your portfolio.

Endowments Are Different

Effective management of a university endowment requires balancing fundamentally competing objectives. On the one hand, the university requires immediate proceeds to support the current generation of scholars. On the other hand, investment managers must consider the needs of generations to come. The endowment must be safeguarded so that it will survive as long as Yale itself, which we believe means forever.
    —President Richard Levin, 2000 Yale endowment report

Endowments are a little different from the average investment portfolio. First of all, they don't have to pay any taxes to the United States government. This enables the endowments to pursue asset classes and strategies that vary from taxable accounts since they do not have to make investment decisions based on considerations of long-term versus short-term capital gains.

Second, endowments have a long-term investment horizon: forever. They hope to exist in perpetuity, trying to treat future generations of students fairly and similarly to the current generation. To do so, endowments typically spend between 4% and 5% of their endowment every year to cover university operating costs.[3] Because of this long-term horizon, endowments have an unrestricted investment policy and do not have the liquidity needs of a normal investor (buying a house, paying for a child's college education, paying for medical bills, and so on). This allows endowments to invest in illiquid asset classes like timber that may require an investment time horizon of more than 20 years.

To keep the endowment from dwindling, the endowment manager aims for portfolio returns that outpace inflation (historically around 3% per year but it has been much higher) and university spending rates (4% to 5%). Inflation is the endowment's worst enemy, and ideally an endowment would like its performance chart to look like Yale's (see Figure 1.2), with the endowment's growth handily outperforming the ravages of inflation over time. Returns before inflation are called nominal returns, while returns after inflation are called real returns.

Endowments are becoming increasingly important to the health of a university, and a sustainable endowment frees the university from relying on any single source of funding. Funds can be used to invest in new facilities, create and maintain academic posts, fund research, and create new scholarships.

---

[3]Politicians have recently gotten involved asserting that the endowments do not spend enough given rising tuition costs. Legislation is being considered that would require endowments to spend a certain percentage of assets per year. This is similar to foundations, which are currently required to spend 5% of assets to maintain their tax-exempt status.

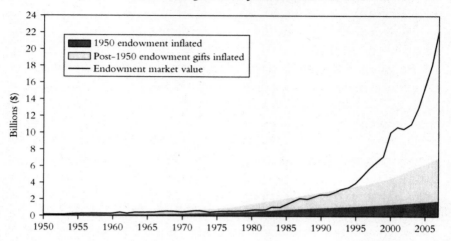

Endowment growth outpaces inflation 1950–2007

Figure 1.2   Yale Endowment vs. Inflation, 1950–2007, Fiscal Year Ending June 30th
Source: Yale 2007 endowment report.

Figure 1.3 details an example of how the Yale endowment proceeds are spent. Yale endowment spending has grown from 12% of the operational budget in 1990 ($86 million) to 33% today ($684 million). If you think that is impressive, almost *half* of Princeton University's operating budget is funded from its endowment.

How Not to Run an Endowment

Harvard, Yale, and Princeton highlight the contributions a strong endowment can make to a university. To illustrate how poor management of endowment assets can hinder a university, here are a few examples of unwise decision making.

In the early 1970s, the University of Rochester had the third largest endowment after Harvard University and the University of Texas. Due to poor returns (including losing 40% in one year), it now ranks 39th. High on the list of unfortunate decisions were large allocations to stocks of local companies like Kodak and

How Not to Run an Endowment (*Continued*)

Xerox. The stocks performed poorly, and the school had to massively downsize its faculty and academic programs in the mid-1990s. (One of the top mistakes that individual investors make is investing all of their money in a local company or an employer's stock. You could get rich, but the risk will be very high—just ask former Enron and Bear Stearns employees.)

The risk in placing the entire endowment portfolio in a concentrated investment is also evident at Emory University, otherwise known as Coke University. We bet you can guess what stock it held almost all of its assets in.

Boston University is another example of excessive risk taking and conflicts of interest. BU had a venture capital subsidiary that invested in 1979 in the private biotech company Seragen, which was founded by scientists affiliated with BU. BU invested over $100 million in Seragen from 1979 until 1997. To contextualize the size of this single investment, the entire BU endowment in 1979 was only $142 million (in 1976 it was only $31 million). Seragen had an initial public offering in 1992, and by late 1997 the $100 million invested by BU was worth only about $4 million. However, by this time the endowment had grown to over $400 million, so while the loss was painful, it was not catastrophic. After overcoming poor performance in the equity bear market from 2000–2003, the endowment has recovered with over $1 billion in assets (Lerner, 2007).

The concentration question is often more acute in the foundation space where many of the assets are typically in the stock of the company that made the foundation possible. The Packard Foundation held nearly 90% of its assets in Hewlett-Packard stock. At the peak of the equity bull market the Packard Foundation was worth over $15 billion, but declined by two-thirds to $5 billion by 2003 and increased to around $6.5 billion at the end of 2007.

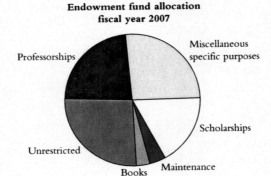

**Operating budget revenue
fiscal year 2007**

Grants and contracts

Tuition, room, board

Medical services

Endowment

Gifts

Other investment income

Other income

Figure 1.3   Yale Endowment Contribution to Operating Budget
SOURCE: 2007 Yale endowment report.

Size Matters . . .

The U.S. endowments manage a lot of money (Table 1.1). The endowments that manage more than $1 billion—what we refer to as the Super Endowments—manage a collective $293 billion.[4] While the 76 Super Endowments make up about 10% of the total 785 endowments, the Super Endowments represent over 70% of all the assets under management.

---

[4] We will also refer to the "dollar-weighted endowments" as "Super Endowments" as they are very similar. The categories for "average endowment" and "equal-weighted endowment" will be used interchangeably.

Table 1.1 Endowment Assets by Size

Endowment Assets	Number of Institutions	Percent of Total Institutions	Total Dollars (billions)	Percent of Total Dollars	Endowment per FTE Student
Greater than $1 Billion	76	9.7%	$293.3	71.3%	$149,986
$500 Million to $1 Billion	65	8.3	45.8	11.1	45,384
$100 Million to $500 Million	232	29.6	54.1	13.2	27,337
$50 Million to $100 Million	156	19.9	11.3	2.7	11,639
$25 Million to $50 Million	126	16.1	4.7	1.1	6,682
Less than $25 Million	130	16.6	1.9	0.5	3,011
Full Sample	**785**	**100.0%**	**$411.2**	**100.0%**	**$56,766**

Source: 2007 NACUBO Endowment Study.

The two largest endowments at the end of 2008 were Harvard with $36.5 billion and Yale with $22.8 billion.

You may be thinking $36 billion is *a lot* of money, but keep in mind that the biggest pension fund, the California Public Employees' Retirement System (CalPERS), manages over $250 billion. The largest mutual fund, the Vanguard 500 Index fund, manages over $120 billion, and both Fidelity and Barclays Global have over $1.5 *trillion* under management.

The average size of an endowment was about $100 million in 1992 versus over $500 million today. Table 1.2 is a list of the top 20 endowments by size for the end of the 2007 endowment fiscal year (usually June 30th).[5] The 2008 NACUBO update was not available at the time of publication.

---

[5]A note to U.K. readers: Start donating to your alma maters! Only Cambridge and Oxford would rank in the top 20 biggest endowments, and then less than 15th. No other U.K. university would fall in the top 150. As an acknowledgment of the importance of the endowment investing office, Yale's David Swensen is now a consultant to Cambridge and both endowments hired their first chief investment officers this past year.

Table 1.2   Top 20 Endowments by Size

Rank	Institution	State	2007 Endowment Funds ($000)
1	Harvard University	MA	$34,634,906
2	Yale University	CT	22,530,200
3	Stanford University	CA	17,164,836
4	Princeton University	NJ	15,787,200
5	University of Texas system	TX	15,613,672
6	MIT	MA	9,980,410
7	Columbia University	NY	7,149,803
8	University of Michigan	MI	7,089,830
9	University of Pennsylvania	PA	6,635,187
10	Texas A&M system	TX	6,590,300
11	Northwestern University	IL	6,503,292
12	University of California	CA	6,439,436
13	University of Chicago	IL	6,204,189
14	University of Notre Dame	IN	5,976,973
15	Duke University	NC	5,910,280
16	Washington University	MO	5,567,843
17	Emory University	GA	5,561,743
18	Cornell University	NY	5,424,733
19	Rice University	TX	4,669,544
20	University of Virginia	VA	4,370,209

Source: 2007 NACUBO Endowment Study.

The average endowment has about $57,000 of assets per student. Compare that figure with the average of $150,000 for the Super Endowments (and over $400,000 for the private Super Endowments), and you can easily see why the schools with larger endowments have a competitive advantage. Princeton has the highest endowment per student ratio for undergraduate schools overall with over $2 million per student. Virginia Military Institute has the highest for public undergraduate schools with $312,000 per student, and The Rockefeller University has the highest for graduate schools with an astonishing $8 million per student.

Grinnell College, a small college in Iowa, now boasts the third largest endowment among liberal arts colleges, and it is in the top 10 overall for endowment assets per student. Grinnell has none other than Warren Buffett to thank—he is a lifetime trustee and advised the endowment to buy a small TV station in Dayton, Ohio for $12.9 million in 1976. Eight years later the endowment sold the station for $50 million, effectively doubling the size of the endowment. Another brilliant move for Grinnell was an early investment in Intel (Intel co-founder Robert Noyce is a Grinnell alum).

. . . and So Does Performance

Now that we have established that the endowments manage a lot of money, how do they perform as a group? Table 1.3 details the 1- to 10-year performance for the Super Endowments versus the average endowment (equal weighted). Over the past 10 years the Super Endowments have returned more than the smaller endowments, 11.1% per year versus 8.4% for the average endowment. Also included in the table are indexes for U.S. stocks (S&P 500), bonds (Lehman Aggregate), inflation (CPI-U), and university inflation (HEPI).[6]

Table 1.3 Rates of Return by Endowment Size

Investment Pool Assets	1-year	3-year	5-year	10-year
Number of Endowments	726	683	636	499
Super Endowments	21.5%	16.8%	14.4%	11.7%
Average Endowment	17.2	12.4	11.1	8.6
S&P 500	20.6	11.7	10.7	7.1
Lehman Bond Aggregate	6.1	4.0	4.5	6.0
CPI-U	2.7	3.2	3.0	2.8
HEPI	3.4	4.0	3.9	3.9

Source: 2007 NACUBO Endowment Study.

---

[6]CPI-U is a proxy for inflation (data are seasonally adjusted). HEPI is the Higher Education Price Index, an inflation index designed specifically for higher education. It measures the average relative level of prices in a fixed basket of goods and services purchased by colleges and universities each year through current fund educational and general expenditures, excluding research.

Table 1.4   Endowment Returns by Year and Size for 2000–2007

	2007	2006	2005	2004	2003	2002	2001	2000
Super Endowments	21.5%	15.3%	13.9%	17.4%	4.7%	−4.2%	−2.7%	23.8%
Average Endowment	17.2	10.7	9.3	15.1	3.0	−6.0	−3.6	13.0

Source: 2007 **NACUBO** Endowment Study.

Not only do the Super Endowments outperform, but they do so consistently every year. Table 1.4 shows that the Super Endowments have outperformed the average endowment every year since 2000.

Figure 1.4 shows how the Super Endowments consistently outperform in every asset class as well. Granted, the large endowments have achieved this advantage partially because of their strong returns, so

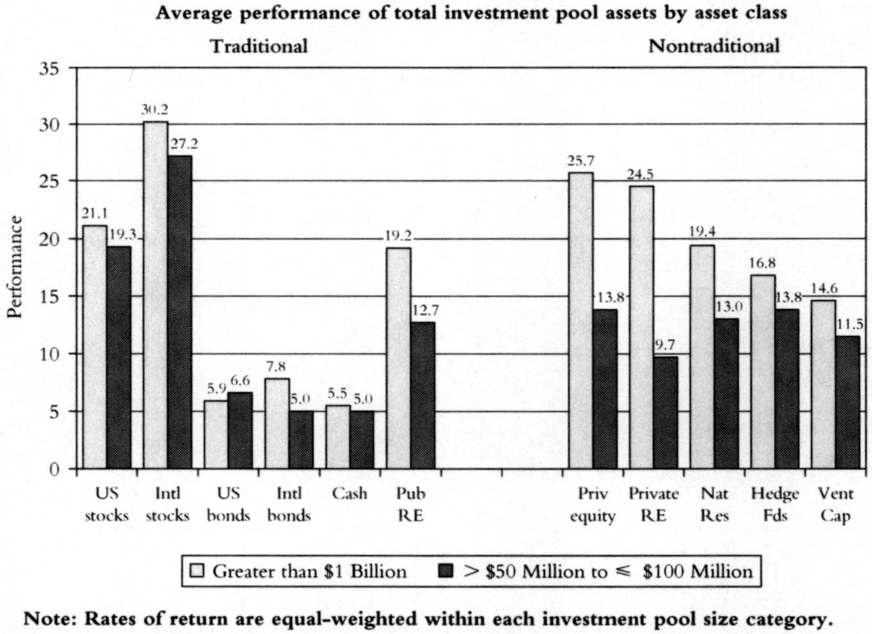

Average performance of total investment pool assets by asset class

Note: Rates of return are equal-weighted within each investment pool size category.

Figure 1.4   Endowment Returns by Asset Class and Size, Fiscal Year Ending June 30th
SOURCE: 2007 **NACUBO** Endowment Study.

there is a bit of the chicken and egg effect. However, because the big endowments outperform every year and in every asset class, there must be more to the story.

So far we have determined that big is better, but why? Figure 1.5 shows the average asset allocation for the Super Endowments and the average endowment. The target asset allocation for an endowment is referred to as the Policy Portfolio. The salient conclusion is that compared with the smaller endowments, the Super Endowments have:

- Fewer stocks (equities).
- Fewer bonds (fixed income).

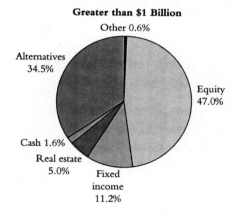

Average asset class allocation of total investment pool assets

Greater than $1 Billion

Other 0.6%
Alternatives 34.5%
Equity 47.0%
Cash 1.6%
Real estate 5.0%
Fixed income 11.2%

> $25 Million to ≤ $100 Million

Alternatives 10.0%   Other 1.4%
Cash 3.5%
Real estate 3.4%
Equity 61.7%
Fixed income 20.3%

Figure 1.5   Endowment Asset Allocations by Size

SOURCE: 2007 NACUBO Endowment Study. Commodities, oil and gas partnerships, and timber are included in the alternatives allocation.

Table 1.5   Changes in Endowment Asset Allocations over Time

Asset Class	1998 Allocation	2007 Allocation	Percent Change
Equity	63.5%	57.6%	−9.3%
Fixed Income	25.6	18.6	−27.3
Real Estate	2.1	3.5	66.7
Cash	4.3	3.5	−18.6
Hedge Funds	2.8	10.6	278.6
Private Equity	0.4	2.3	475.0
Venture Capital	0.7	0.9	28.6
Natural Resources	0.2	1.6	700.0
Other	0.4	1.4	250.0

Source: 2007 NACUBO Endowment Study.

- More real assets (real estate, timber, and commodities).
- More alternatives (hedge funds, private equity, and venture capital).

The trend of all endowments from a traditional allocation toward a more unconventional portfolio has happened over time, and can be seen in Table 1.5 as endowments have decreased their allocation in stocks and bonds while increasing their allocations to real assets and alternatives. Much of this shift has occurred as a response to the great success of the Super Endowments. It is difficult for the smaller endowments to hire and pay for an investing staff, and many have found that outsourcing their management to an investment firm like Investure, Morgan Creek, or Makena Capital makes sense.

Active Management over Passive

So far we have found that the large endowments perform better and they have less traditional portfolios. The Super Endowments are also more active in the management of their funds than smaller endowments. The term active management refers to security selection and market timing rather than a buy-and-hold indexing approach. An academic paper has shown that the more active endowments perform better, and that their active security selection skills—not asset allocation—is the most important factor in determining the *relative* performance between endowments (Brown, 2007).[7] The Super Endowments actively manage almost all of their investments at approximately 95%.

We will examine the methods the Super Endowments utilize to actively manage their portfolios in the upcoming chapters.

The Super Endowments also have a few advantages versus the smaller ones:

- **Pricing advantage**—If an endowment is considering allocating a large chunk of cash to an outside fund, the endowment will likely have leverage in negotiating down external management fees.
- **Loyal alumni**—Many alumni remain loyal to their alma mater. The managers who go on to manage top tier funds may offer favorable terms or keep their funds open to their alma mater's endowment when closed to normal investors. Long-standing relationships guarantee a "seat at the table."
- **Dedicated staff**—Even though their salaries are less than what the endowment managers and analysts would make in the hedge fund industry, the Super Endowments are large enough to employ a staff dedicated to managing the endowment, a luxury the small endowments do not have.
- **Relationships**—The Super Endowments have had dedicated investment offices operating for decades. The relationships and industry knowledge that have been developed over the years are important sources of excess return.

In short, the Super Endowments have several advantages over their small endowment counterparts, including superior active management, access to better internal and external management talent, pricing leverage, and other common advantages of scale. While the majority of

---

[7]This finding is consistent with evidence on pension and mutual funds, which finds that passive asset allocation is the most important determinant of the level and variation of endowment returns over time, but it is the active management that is the most important factor in determining a fund's *relative* standing within the group. (Brinson, Hood, and Beebower (1986), and Ibbotson and Kaplan (2000)).

the Ivy League universities have similar Policy Portfolio allocations, we will focus on the two largest as case studies in the next two chapters.

Summary

- Endowment assets under management are large and growing.
- Endowments have several advantages over the investing public: They are tax-exempt, have long-term time horizons, and have few investment restrictions.
- A large and strongly performing endowment gives the school a huge competitive advantage, and contributes substantial amounts to the school's operating budget.
- Poor management of the endowment can be detrimental to the operations and survival of a university.
- The biggest endowments, known as the Super Endowments, perform better than the smaller endowments, and do so year in and year out in every asset class.
- The Super Endowments employ a less traditional asset allocation—more real assets and alternatives, and fewer U.S. stocks and bonds.
- The Super Endowments utilize their active asset management capabilities (market timing and security selection), relationships, and pricing leverage to outperform the smaller endowments.

Chapter 2

The Yale Endowment

Those who can, do. Those who can't, teach.
—H. L. MENCKEN

The author of this quotation never heard of David Swensen. Swensen graduated from the University of Wisconsin in 1975 with a major in economics, followed by a Ph.D. also in economics from Yale University under the Nobel Laureate James Tobin. Swensen is now a professor himself teaching classes at Yale, and has authored two best-selling books. Sounds like the typical ivory tower career path, right?

Except for the past 22 years Swensen has also managed the Yale University endowment. Since Swensen took over the reins of the Yale endowment in 1985 it has returned more than 16% per year. To put that figure into perspective, the S&P 500 Index has returned about 12% in one of the greatest bull markets in United States history.

Even more impressive, Swensen has accomplished this feat with 33% less volatility than the S&P 500. The Yale endowment recorded a worst year of only −0.20% versus −17.99% for the S&P 500. Equally impressive, the most cited measure of risk-adjusted returns, the Sharpe Ratio, is more than double that of the S&P 500. These returns place Yale in the top 1% of all institutional managers.

The endowment's contributions to the Yale operating budget have increased from 10% of overall revenues in 1985, to 33% today. Swensen's outperformance over the returns of the average endowment (over $11 billion and counting) has done more to bolster Yale as an institution than any other source or donor. How did Yale happen to find one of the best portfolio managers of all time and become the investment powerhouse it is today?

The Yale endowment hasn't always been in great standing. This chapter takes a brief look at the history of the endowment before examining the theory, process, and discipline Swensen uses to manage the portfolio today.

History of the Endowment

Yale was founded in 1701 by a group of clergymen and supported by the General Assembly of the Colony of Connecticut for nearly two centuries. The endowment was established when James Fitch donated 637 acres of land in 1701, and Yale received various grants and funds from numerous other sources including property, books and materials, and even nine bales of goods by Elihu Yale to secure naming rights in 1718. For the first 100 years most of the donations came in the form of random goods, property, and land.

In the early 1800s, two trustees along with the Yale treasurer founded the Eagle Bank of New Haven. In addition to their own money, the men invested most of the endowment in the stock of the new bank (talk about a conflict of interest!). By 1825 the bank was in bankruptcy, and over 90% of the endowment fund was lost. In response, the first endowment fund-raising effort occurred in 1831, and the campaign raised over $100,000 to secure a permanent endowment.

During the rest of the 1800s the portfolio was largely invested in bonds. In 1856, bonds comprised 71% of the portfolio, with real estate and stocks accounting for 16% and 13%, respectively. By 1900, the endowment totaled $5.3 million, and the portfolio was allocated with bonds at 64%, real estate at 22%, and stocks at 13%. Right in line with the equity run-up of the 1920s, the mix moved toward a 42% allocation to equities by 1929, and the losses following the stock market crash resulted in a two-thirds allocation to bonds for the next 30 years.[1]

Beginning in 1952, endowment management began to be transformed by a series of important events. First, Harry Markowitz's seminal 1952 paper "Portfolio Selection" explained the benefits of portfolio diversification. In addition to earning Markowitz a Nobel Prize in Economics, this Modern Portfolio Theory enabled managers to quantify with mathematics the benefits of not putting all of your eggs in one basket.

This paper was followed by the Ford Foundation's annual report that argued for additional shifts in portfolio management theory. The Ford Foundation's head, McGeorge Bundy, advocated less caution and more of a focus on total return—not simply income from bonds as the basis of foundation and endowment management. In 1971, the Ford Foundation seeded the nonprofit Commonfund with $2.8 million to professionally pool and manage endowment assets. (The Commonfund now has more than 1,500 institutions as clients and over $35 billion in assets under management.) Finally, the 1972 Uniform Management of Institutional Funds Act clarified how institutions could invest with the goal of total return in mind.

These events allowed for the eventual move of endowment portfolios toward more optimal asset allocations, but in the interim it simply led to the funds shifting more of their assets into U.S. stocks. Yale was no exception, and after another large run-up in stocks, the Yale trustees decided belatedly to increase their allocation to stocks, as they had prior to the 1929 crash. The trustees outsourced management to a private firm they established called Endowment Management and

---

[1]Not everyone was devastated by the crash. Dean Mathey was the chairman of the investment committee of Princeton University in the late 1920s, and realizing the speculative excesses going on around him, moved the endowment out of stocks and into bonds. The move proved ill-timed for a year but once the crash of 1929 hit, the endowment was protected from the greater than 80% loss in stocks. Mathey waited another 14 years for an opportunity and then moved the endowment back into an allocation of 80% stocks. When chastised for being reckless with the endowment (it was a widely held belief at the time that bonds were the only conservative choice for an endowment), he replied, "The only true test of conservatism is to be right in the future." Well said sir! (Knowlton, 1987).

Research Corporation (EM&R), which was jointly owned by Yale and the officers of the fund. EM&R was then allowed to manage outside money as well (similar to the hybrid model Mark Yusko[2] attempted when he was at the University of North Carolina). While this focus on equity like assets was beneficial over the long run, the immediate timing could not have been worse with U.S. stocks experiencing a 40% decline in the 1973–1974 bear market.

The 1960s and 1970s were disastrous for the Yale endowment as the forces of a stagnant stock market and increasing inflation combined to drive down the real after-inflation market value of the endowment. The increased allocation to equities, particularly growth stocks, pulled the endowment's inflation adjusted value down by half and left the endowment significantly below the trustees' target. Using the rearview mirror to drive can lead to poor investing decisions; in later chapters we will examine some of the behavioral biases that led the Yale trustees to make unfortunately timed decisions and how you can avoid them in your own portfolio.

Figure 2.1 shows the poorly performing endowment's effects on the diminished contributions to the overall revenue of the university. Once accounting for around 50% of university revenue, the endowment income of the 1960s and 1970s added only minimal amounts to the operating budget.

As recently as 1982, the endowment was still below the targeted purchasing power goal. Yale ended the relationship with EM&R and the mix slowly moved toward the traditional 60%/40% stock/bond mix. By the time David Swensen joined in 1985, the allocation looked like Table 2.1, with about 62% in U.S. stocks, 6% in foreign stocks, 10% in bonds, and 9% in real assets.[3] A bull market in all things financial, coupled with declining inflation (and Swensen's arrival) helped propel the endowment to almost three times the purchasing power target today.

---

[2]Mark Yusko used to manage the University of North Carolina endowment. He attempted the hybrid model, but due to university blowback, left to found his own company Morgan Creek. There are very good interviews with Yusko in *Hedge Hunters* and *Foundation and Endowment Investing*.

[3]Absolute return is a phrase Swensen coined, and we use it interchangeably with the hedge fund category throughout the book.

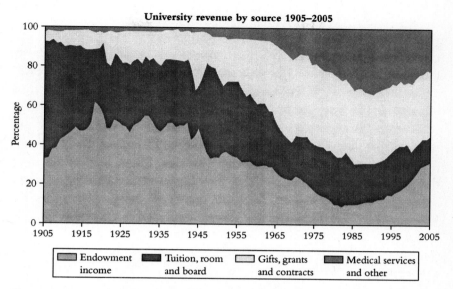

Figure 2.1   Endowment Contribution to University Revenue
SOURCE: 2005 Yale endowment report.

Table 2.1   Asset Allocation Targets of Yale

	1985	1990	1995	2000	2005
U.S. Stocks	61.6%	48.0%	21.8%	14.2%	14.1%
Foreign Stocks	6.3	15.2	12.5	9.0	13.7
Bonds	10.3	21.2	12.2	9.4	3.8
Cash	10.1	0.9	1.8	8.1	1.9
Real Assets	8.5	8.0	13.5	14.9	25.0
Private Equity	3.2	6.7	17.2	25.0	14.8
Absolute Return	0.0	0.0	21.0	19.5	25.7

Source: 2005 Yale endowment report. Oil and gas and forestland were included in private equity until 1998, thereafter in real assets.

The asset allocation mix Swensen envisioned—in what he called an "uncomfortably idiosyncratic portfolio"—didn't firmly take root until the early 1990s. The allocation changed dramatically under Swensen's leadership, and next we take a look at how he was able to alter the course of Yale history.[4]

---

[4]Swensen gives significant credit to Dean Takahashi for his contributions to the management of the Yale endowment.

David Swensen's Ascent

David Swensen graduated from the University of Wisconsin in 1975 with a degree in economics. He then attended Yale and received his Ph.D. under the legendary Nobel Laureate James Tobin (his doctoral dissertation focused on the eponymous "Tobin's Q"). Upon graduation, he worked at Salomon Brothers for a three-year stint, where he structured the first financial swap transaction in history between IBM and the World Bank.

After a brief time at Lehman Brothers, Tobin offered Swensen the position of managing the Yale Investment Office (YIO), to which Swensen famously replied, "I don't know anything about portfolio management." Tobin countered, "That doesn't matter. We always thought you were a smart guy and Yale needs you" (*Capital Ideas Evolving*).

Swensen agreed to an 80% cut in pay, and while he now makes a little over $1 million a year, he could be earning many times that amount managing a hedge fund or a fund of funds in the private sector.

Swensen is clearly motivated by factors more meaningful than a large Wall Street paycheck. "I had a great time on Wall Street, but it didn't satisfy my soul," he says. "And I've always loved educational institutions. My father was a university professor, my grandfather was a university professor. So there must be something in the genes" (NPR, *All Things Considered*).

How did David Swensen go about constructing this portfolio that was so far removed from commonly accepted allocations of the day?

The Yale portfolio is constructed based on academic theory—namely a framework known as mean-variance analysis. The technique was originally developed by Harry Markowitz in concert with Swensen's mentor Tobin, and eventually earned Markowitz a Nobel Prize in 1990. It really boils down to "don't put all your eggs in one basket," or in other words, diversification works. You can put together a bunch of risky assets (stocks, real estate, commodities) and as long as they don't all move together in a correlated fashion, the combined portfolio is less risky than the individual parts. Roger Gibson has some great examples of multiasset-class investing in his academic papers and his book, *Asset Allocation*, and we will take up the topic in more detail in Chapter 4.

Mean-variance analysis uses the expected returns of various asset classes, the expected risk (volatility, or how much an asset bounces around), and the expected correlation to find the portfolios with the highest return for a given level of risk (or lowest risk for a given level

Mean Variance for Beginners

For those who have never heard of mean-variance analysis, do not lose faith. Think about it this way. Let's say you are baking chocolate chip cookies (your portfolio). You mainly need butter, flour, chocolate chips, eggs, baking soda, and sugar (the various asset classes). There are lots of different ways to combine these ingredients, and the mix will be based on individual taste (risk and return preferences). Maybe the cook is a diabetic, so he would make sugar free cookies (no high-tech stocks). Some people don't like too many chocolate chips, and so their mix of ingredients will be different from someone who likes lots of chocolate chips. There are lots of different mixes (portfolios) possible, but for the most part there is a most efficient mix for each person. If you completely leave out certain ingredients, your outcome will be less than optimal. And if you eat all the cookie dough (spend all your money), you will never get to enjoy and share the cookies with your loved ones.

of return). A correlation of +1.0 means that two assets have a perfect positive relationship (they move together), and −1.0 means that they have a perfect negative relationship (they move opposite one another).

Figure 2.2 is a basic chart showing numerous asset classes and the curved line known as the efficient frontier.[5] Portfolios situated on the curved line have the highest return for a given level of risk (and vice versa).

This framework often leads to overweighting assets with low (or negative) correlation to the existing portfolio, such as real assets and hedge funds.[6] One of the problems with mean variance analysis is that

---

[5]If you really want to get deep on this subject Google "risk parity" for the papers by Bridgewater and PanAgora (which will also be linked on this book's web site www.theivyportfolio.com).

[6]It does not make sense to label real assets as alternative asset classes. Humans have been buying and selling land and commodities far longer than they have traded shares of IBM. Hedge funds are not a separate asset class, but rather funds that trade existing asset classes. More on this in Chapters 4 and 6.

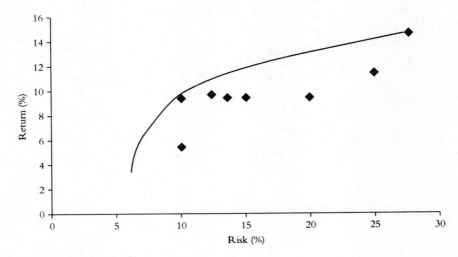

Figure 2.2   Efficient Frontier

it is very dependent on the inputs. It is very simple to use historical market returns as they are a fact. The mean variance optimization will tell you what the best allocation is for the *past*. We care about the best allocation in the *future*.

For example, there is a very interesting piece on market history from the *Global Financial Data Guide to Total Returns*. Looking at historical data from capital asset returns in the 1800s, Dr. Bryan Taylor finds that:

- Most people invested in bonds, not stocks.
- Virtually all of an equity investor's returns came in the form of dividends, not capital gains.
- There was little difference in the returns to stocks and bonds.
- Since the government did not issue treasury bills and deposits were not federally insured, there was no "risk free" investment available to investors.
- Bond and dividend yields declined over the course of the century as the risk to investors and inflation declined.
- Although prices rose and fell in any given year, from 1815 to 1914, there was no overall inflation in the US and in most countries on the Gold Standard.

Taylor states, "What is interesting about these points, which would have been taken as given before 1914, is that during the twentieth century none of these assumptions proved to be true. By the end of the twentieth century, most investors were investing in stocks, not bonds, depended on capital gains, not dividends, received a large premium on stocks over bonds, had risk-free investment alternatives, saw interest rates rise during most of the twentieth century, and suffered from the worst inflation in human history."

A mean variance optimization performed at the beginning of the twentieth century would have resulted in far different results than one performed at the beginning of the twenty-first century. Assumptions that you may be using today as fact (stocks outperform bonds, small caps outperform large caps, etc), could prove to be unreliable in the future.

Will stocks return 10% going forward? How volatile are commodities going to be over the next 50 years? Has private equity seen its day in the sun? Will foreign stocks become more correlated to domestic stocks? As Niels Bohr said, "Prediction is very difficult, especially about the future."

While expected returns and expected volatilities are difficult to forecast, correlations are even harder. Combining assets with correlations that are all over the map does little to help your portfolio. The best way to go about the process is to combine assets with consistently low correlations to reduce risk.[7] Table 2.2 shows that commodities have the least correlation with traditional asset classes over the long term.

While this table is useful, the process is made more difficult because correlations change depending on the market environment.

Ray Dalio, founder of the $150 billion hedge fund group Bridgewater Associates, expresses his opinion in the book *2020 Vision*: "We don't assume stable correlations, we look at a range of past correlations to stress-test our portfolio based on different correlation assumptions and we structure our portfolios to have no unintended consequences that would favor one type of economic environment over another."

As an example that correlations can (and do) change, Figure 2.3 charts the three-year rolling correlations of stocks and bonds since 1903.

---

[7]Want more information on this subject? Read *Mastering the Art of Asset Allocation*, which has 174 pages on the correlations of asset classes. William Coaker also has two papers in a series titled "The Volatility of Correlation" and "Emphasizing Low Correlated Assets" that have great tables of lots of asset classes and the distributions of correlations. The links to these and other papers can be found at www.theivyportfolio.com.

Table 2.2   Correlations of Annual Total Returns, 1973–2008

	U.S. Stocks	Foreign Stocks	U.S. Bonds	Commodities	Real Estate
U.S. Stocks	1.00	0.66	0.15	−0.09	0.59
Foreign Stocks	0.66	1.00	−0.04	−0.01	0.38
U.S. Bonds	0.15	−0.04	1.00	−0.21	0.08
Commodities	−0.09	−0.01	−0.21	1.00	−0.17
Real Estate	0.59	0.38	0.08	−0.17	1.00
Average	0.33	0.25	−0.01	−0.12	0.22

Source: U.S. Stocks—S&P 500, Foreign Stocks—MSCI EAFE, Commodities—GSCI, Real Estate—REITs, U.S. Bonds—10-Year Treasury.

(This measures the correlation between stocks and bonds, updated every month using only the past three years of monthly returns.) While on average stocks and bonds are not very correlated with each other at .15, the correlation has varied from −.61 to .62 (and the one-year rolling correlation from −.85 to .86).

Table 2.3 shows the one-year rolling correlations between the main asset classes and U.S. stocks. On average U.S. stocks are only partially correlated to foreign stocks and Real Estate Investment Trusts (REITs), and less so to U.S. government bonds and commodities. However, over any one 12-month period the returns can be nearly identical. The takeaway is

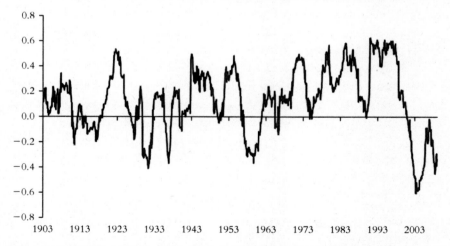

Figure 2.3   3-Year Rolling Correlation of the S&P 500 and 10-Year U.S. Government Bonds 1903-2008

Table 2.3 One-Year Rolling Correlations, 1973–2008

	Correlation with the S&P 500		
	Average	Maximum	Minimum
Foreign Stocks	0.54	0.96	−0.41
U.S. Bonds	0.20	0.86	−0.85
Commodities	0.01	0.95	−0.79
Real Estate	0.55	0.97	−0.30

Source: U.S. Stocks—S&P 500, Foreign Stocks—MSCI EAFE, Commodities—GSCI, Real Estate—REITs, U.S. Bonds—10-Year Treasury.

that even though some asset classes are on average negatively correlated with one another, in the short run they can move together almost identically. This matters little over the very long run, but for individuals looking to project their financial situation over the next 1 to 10 years, there are significant implications. Over the short term anything can happen as evidenced by nearly every asset class declining in 2008. This is one reason why risk management is so important—more in Chapter 7.

Correlations should be viewed as a tendency, not an absolute, and they are certainly something you cannot count on. A famous Wall Street saying is that in times of economic shocks, all correlations go to 1! (Meaning when it hits the fan, everything goes down together.)

Yale also uses a technique called Monte Carlo simulation, which stress tests the portfolio over thousands of different scenarios to come up with a range of likely outcomes. This simulation can give insight into the most likely outcome, as well as the chances of best- and worst-case occurring scenarios. (The moniker Monte Carlo was coined by U.S. physics researchers in the 1940s as a reference to the repetitive nature and randomness of possible outcomes in a gambling casino.)

Another way to stress test these correlations is to look at the returns when equities had their worst months. Table 2.4 shows the 10 worst months in stocks since 1972 and the returns of the other asset classes in those months.

The performance of foreign stocks and REITs did very little to dampen the losses from U.S. stocks. Only bonds did a good job of performing strongly in the months when stocks did poorly and did so nearly all of the time.

Table 2.4   Average Performance of Asset Classes during
the Worst 10 Stock Market Months 1972–2008

	Average	% Positive
S&P 500	−12.28%	0%
Foreign Stocks	−12.11	0
U.S. Bonds	1.94	90
Commodities	−2.24	50
Real Estate	−9.05	10

Source: U.S. Stocks—S&P 500, Foreign Stocks—MSCI EAFE, Commodities—
GSCI, Real Estate—REITs, US Bonds—10-Year Treasury.

These mathematical techniques are useful to gain perspective, but they have other problems such as accounting for structural changes in markets and modeling liquidity and rare low-probability events (as evidenced by the 2007 herding/liquidity-based quantitative equity hedge fund meltdown). The 2007 Yale endowment report reads, "Investment management involves art as much as science."

These methods, as well as a little common sense and experience, lead Yale to the current Policy Portfolio for 2007. The Policy Portfolio is simply their target portfolio for the year. See Table 2.5. (A more detailed Policy Portfolio follows later in this chapter; we included this simplified version to compare Yale's endowment to the average endowment.)

Yale does not break out its investments in real assets. We have assumed an even split between real estate and commodities, but in reality the university has a diverse allocation of timber, oil and gas partnerships, real estate investments, and other real assets.

Compared with the average endowment, Yale has:

- Less stock exposure.
- Much less bond exposure.
- Much more real estate, commodities, private equity, and hedge funds.

The portfolio reaches for high returns, thus the endowment is biased towards equity, and equity-like asset classes, which total 96% of the endowment. Bonds, due to their vulnerability to inflation, are in the

Table 2.5   Yale Policy Portfolio (2007)

	Yale	Average Endowment
Stocks	26.0%	57.6%
Bonds	4.0	18.6
Real Estate	14.0	3.5
Commodities	14.0	1.6
Private Equity	19.0	3.2
Hedge Funds	23.0	10.6
Cash	0.0	3.5
Other	0.0	1.4
Total	**100.0%**	**100.0%**

Source: 2007 Yale endowment report.

portfolio only as a hedge against deflation. Yale has a large allocation to real assets and nontraditional asset classes due to their return potential and diversifying power. The long-term time horizon (forever) is suited to exploiting illiquid and less efficient markets such as venture capital, leveraged buyouts, oil and gas, timber, and real estate.

This target mix is expected to produce returns after inflation of 6.3% with risk (volatility) of 12.4%. The Yale 2007 endowment report states that their measure of inflation is "based on a basket of goods and services specific to higher education that tends to exceed the Consumer Price Index (CPI) by approximately one percentage point." The Commonfund, a nonprofit devoted to management of college and university endowments, tracks an index called the Higher Education Price Index (HEPI). It ended the 2007 year at 3.4%, roughly 1% above the CPI figure of 2.6%.

When you add the HEPI inflation numbers back into the above numbers it results in an expected return target of 9.7%, with volatility of 12.4%. See Table 2.6.

While Yale uses this table as its bogey return to beat, it attempts to outperform this allocation using active management.

Table 2.6 Yale Endowment Expected Returns and Risk

Yale Expected Returns and Risk	Target Return after Inflation	Target Return before Inflation	Target Risk
U.S. Stocks	6.0%	9.4%	20.0%
Foreign Developed Stocks	6.0	9.4	20.0
Foreign Emerging Stocks	8.0	11.4	25.0
Bonds	2.0	5.4	10.0
Real Assets	6.0	9.4	13.6
Absolute Return (Event Driven)	6.0	9.4	10.0
Absolute Return (Value Driven)	6.0	9.4	15.0
Private Equity	11.2	14.6	27.7
Portfolio Total	**6.3%**	**9.7%**	**12.4%**

Source: 2007 Yale endowment report.

Of Alphas and Betas

Rewarding investments tend to hide in dark corners, not in the glare of floodlights.

—2005 YALE ANNUAL REPORT

Financial professionals love jargon. They like to refer to benchmark indexes and asset classes as beta.[8] All this means is that the investor buys something and gets paid for holding systematic risk. Asset classes like stocks have higher expected returns than cash (over the long run) because of the simple reason that they are more risky. Over the very long run risky assets will return more than less risky assets, but not too much or they will attract a flood of money thus bidding up prices and lowering future returns.

An asset class or index can be regarded as beta if it can be described simply and is easy to invest in. The S&P 500 is a simple example of U.S. stock market beta. Anyone can replicate the index, and fees to invest in

---

[8]This is a newer interpretation of the word beta. Per Markowitz, the classical definition was that the value of beta measures the sensitivity of a security's return to the market portfolio.

it should be very low. The Goldman Sachs Commodity Index (GSCI) is an example of commodity beta.

For a strategy to be regarded as beta, its fees should be inexpensive (think Vanguard funds and exchange-traded funds (ETFs) that cost less than 0.5% a year), it should be easy to copy (think of the 10,000 mutual funds) and simple to understand. Clifford Asness, founder of AQR Capital, has defined beta as "any strategy that can be written down" (Idzorek, 2006).

Then there is alpha. Alpha is the value added by a portfolio manager by active management (and is usually measured against some benchmark index, or beta). Think of the skill-based returns added by Warren Buffett versus the S&P 500, or the returns of PIMCO's Bill Gross versus the Lehman Aggregate Bond Index. A fund manager can either create positive alpha (good picks) or negative alpha (bad picks). Alpha is a zero sum game, meaning for one person to win someone else has to lose. (Actually it is negative sum when you include transaction commissions and slippage.) Alpha is much harder to find and is constantly changing. Investors are much more willing to pay large fees for this rare and elusive alpha. Finding alpha requires the active management of a portfolio.

It is hard to distinguish some of these simple beta factors from skill-based alpha. Previous sources of alpha that have been commoditized as systematic beta factors are value versus growth, convertible arbitrage strategies, and managed futures strategies. An investor should not pay high fees to a manager who is simply replicating cheaper sources of beta.

Yale's target Policy Portfolio is an example of a passive, indexed portfolio return made up of various market betas (with the exception of the alternatives that are difficult to index). Indexing assures the investor of the market return, but offers no opportunity to outperform the markets. However, Yale's is not an ordinary portfolio.

Yale uses active management techniques and focuses on the areas where there is the most value to add for active management—where the markets are the least efficient. (There's no talk of completely efficient markets in this ivory tower.) As can be seen in Tables 2.7 and 2.8,[9]

---

[9]Quartile is a statistics term that divides a data set into four parts so that each part represents 25% of the population. Top quartile refers to the top 25% of the data.

Table 2.7 Dispersion of Active Management Returns (Asset Returns by Quartile, 10 Years Ending June 30, 2005)

Asset Class	First Quartile	Median	Third Quartile	Range
U.S. Bonds	7.2%	6.9%	6.7%	0.5%
U.S. Large Cap Stocks	11.3	10.4	9.4	2.0
U.S. Small Cap Stocks	15.3	13.2	10.5	4.7
International Stocks	9.7	8.2	5.7	4.0
Absolute Return	15.6	12.5	8.5	7.1
Real Estate	17.6	12.0	8.4	9.3
Leveraged Buyouts	13.3	8.0	−0.4	13.7
Venture Capital	28.7	−1.4	−14.5	43.2

Source: 2005 Yale endowment report.

Table 2.8 Yale vs. Asset Class Benchmarks

	Return	Outperformance
U.S. Stocks	13.50%	5.80%
Foreign Stocks	16.90	6.80
Bonds	6.40	0.60
Real Assets	21.50	11.50
Private Equity	33.90	19.20
Absolute Return	13.10	2.50

Source: Yale 2007 endowment report.

the asset classes with the greatest dispersion of returns are the areas that Yale focuses most of its time in active management.

The tiny range of returns in bonds suggests that it is one of the most efficient markets in the world. Traveling down the market efficiency chart reveals that the best use of a manager's time is attempting to find the top managers in private equity, where the rewards are bountiful. Finding a top manager in fixed income would only add 0.3% per annum excess returns over the median fund while selecting a top venture capital manager would add over 30% excess returns over the median fund per year! In *Pioneering Portfolio Management*, Swensen wrote:

> An inverse relationship exists between efficiency in asset pricing and appropriate degree of active management. Passive management strategies suit highly-efficient markets, such as U.S. Treasury bonds, where market returns drive results and active management adds less than nothing to returns. Active management strategies fit inefficient markets, such as private equity, where market returns contribute very little to ultimate results and investment selection provides the fundamental source of return.

Table 2.8 is a good indication of the previous theoretical discussion. Over the past 10 years Yale has achieved the majority of its absolute outperformance in private equity and real assets.

That is some amazing outperformance! (In fact, there is even a Harvard Business School case study updated every couple of years that focuses on the Yale endowment titled "Yale University Investments Office" by Professors Josh Lerner and Jay Light.) Consistent with the previous observation, Yale has the most outperformance in the least efficient asset classes. It is possible that Yale could become a victim of its own success as more and more institutions follow the "Yale model." The markets will become more and more efficient in those asset classes as money flows in. The low hanging fruit in real assets and private equity will diminish. In the book *2020 Vision*, Bob Litterman of Goldman Sachs is quoted as saying, "I am not worried that markets are fully efficient—yet. But they are becoming more efficient all the time—and fast. The world is going quant, and there are no secrets! Alpha is in limited supply and hard to find."

Outlining the Yale Process

In this section we detail how Yale approaches each asset class. Table 2.9 shows how Yale allocates its assets across eight asset classes. Yale is diligent about maintaining its Policy Portfolio targets, and it rebalances frequently as the positions deviate from the intended targets.

Table 2.9   Yale 2007 Policy Portfolio

	Yale
Domestic Stocks	11%
Foreign Developed Stocks	6
Foreign Emerging Stocks	9
Domestic Bonds	4
Real Estate	14
Commodities	14
Private Equity	19
Hedge Funds	23
Cash	0
Total	**100%**

Source: 2007 Yale endowment report.

Domestic Equity

Although Yale acknowledges that the U.S. stock market is very efficient, it still pursues active management strategies based on bottom-up fundamental stock analysis and security selection. The portfolio consists of specialists running highly concentrated sector portfolios that may look nothing like the stock indices. Such an approach guarantees deviation from the benchmark, and as Figure 2.4 shows, the Yale allocation to equity managers underperformed the market from 1995–2000 before reverting and pulling ahead after the 2000–2003 bear market. The portfolio has a value and small cap bias, two factors that have shown to historically add excess returns. One explanation for the excess returns is that the small cap market is less followed by research analysts and investment firms and thus less efficient than its large cap counterpart. As William Sharpe said in an interview with *Advisor Perspectives* on October 16, 2007:

> To find superior managers, you must look for those with some degree of flexibility. But, in doing so, you will undoubtedly find some managers that are inferior. To beat an index you can't be too close to it, but that is not a guarantee that you will succeed. Whether managers should get a broader mandate depends on their knowledge of the markets.

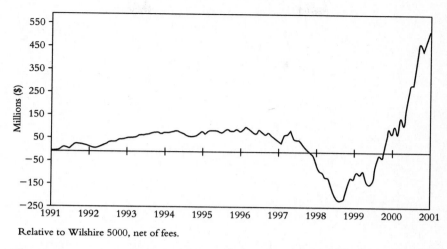

Relative to Wilshire 5000, net of fees.

Figure 2.4   Cumulative Value Added by Yale Domestic Equity Managers (1991–2001)
SOURCE: Yale annual report.

Yale targets its stock portfolio to achieve a return of 9.4% with volatility of 20%. The benchmark Yale uses is the Wilshire 5000 Index.

Foreign Equity

Yale targets a 6% allocation to both foreign developed countries and foreign emerging countries, with a 3% allocation to opportunistic positions. Because the opportunistic positions are expected to be concentrated in emerging markets, we lumped them in with the emerging allocation. Foreign developed includes countries such as Germany and Japan, while emerging would include countries such as India and Brazil.

The active management strategy is similar to the domestic portfolio, with a focus on bottom-up fundamental stock selection. The managers tend to have a regional focus, as well as a focus on the less efficient small cap and emerging markets.

Figure 2.5 shows the cumulative value these managers have added to the endowment. Yale also manages a pool of internal funds that trade closed-end funds. One of the least efficient areas of the market, closed-end funds can and do trade at wide discounts and premiums to their

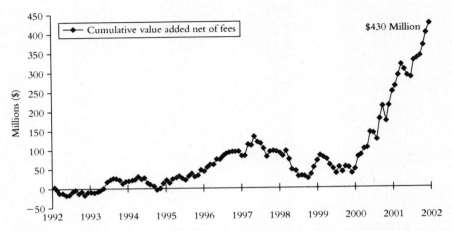

Figure 2.5 Foreign Equities AddValue Relative to Composite Benchmark (1992–2002)

SOURCE: Yale annual report.

net asset value (NAV).[10] Yale indicates it can add "incremental value by purchasing at wide discounts and selling at narrower discounts." For an example of a fund that trades irrationally around its NAV take a look at the historical premiums and discounts of the Herzfeld Caribbean Basin Fund (CUBA) which have ranged from 20% discounts to 100% premiums to NAV. No efficient market here! There are also a few funds that focus on investing in closed-end funds at a discount. The first is the Claymore Goldman Sachs CEF ETN (GCE). The fund targets about 75 holdings, and weights them based on discount to NAV among other factors. Cohen and Steers also has the Closed-End Opportunity Fund (FOF). The fund is structured as a closed-end fund itself, which allows for a double-dip on any potential discounts.

Another interesting observation is that Yale does not hedge currency exposure. This is an area of debate among asset allocation professionals. Yale's position is that currency positions are not expected to add value, improve diversification, or reduce risk.

The foreign equity portfolio has expected returns of 9.4% with volatility of 20% for foreign developed, and 11.4% with volatility of 25% for emerging markets. The benchmark is a composite of 40% MSCI EAFE, 40% MSCI EEM, and 20% opportunistic (HEPI plus 8%).

---

[10]Etfconnect.com is a great resource for researching closed-end funds.

Fixed-Income

The main purpose of the bond portfolio is to act as a hedge against financial accidents or unexpected deflation. Yale finds the assets unattractive due to the low historical and expected returns, as well as the high degree of market efficiency. Swensen argues against allocations to foreign bonds due to their low expected returns and foreign currency exposure.

Yale manages the entire bond portfolio in-house, and it has produced benchmark beating returns consistently. Yale expects the bond portfolio to return 5.4% with volatility of 10%, and the benchmark is the Lehman Brothers U.S. Treasury Index.

Real Assets

Yale still receives investment income from properties donated to the university as far back as the eighteenth century (thanks King George III!). Yale began to make its first oil and gas and commercial real estate investments in the 1950s. In addition to real estate and oil and gas, Yale invests in timberland. All of these real assets are relatively illiquid.

These assets perform well in inflationary environments, and are in relatively inefficient markets. Real assets are a great source of diversification to a traditional portfolio, and Yale has a much larger allocation than the average endowment (28% versus around 10%). Yale prefers to look for active managers with deep operational experience as well as a focus on a particular geographical region or sector. Yale also requires all managers to make a participating investment in every deal so that the managers have some of their own skin in the game. Yale supports emerging managers who do not have huge amounts of assets under management and prefers to build close and long-term relationships.

Yale prefers real estate that generates a current cash yield to reduce the exposure to holding periods and valuation risk, and Yale attempts to locate a majority of its holdings in supply constrained areas. One of the university's early investments in real estate was an office building in Manhattan in which it purchased a 50% interest in 1978 for $47 million (with the remaining interest purchased in 1994). Upon selling the property in 2002, Yale realized nearly a 20% annual return on the investment.

In the oil and gas arena, Yale prefers investments with high quality proven reserves. Yale looks for managers with smaller amounts of assets under management who can source and operate assets more efficiently than larger companies. With timberland, Yale focuses on slow-growing and sustainable management of natural forest properties in the United States.

Yale expects the benchmark to return 9.4% with volatility of 13.6%, and the benchmark is the HEPI + 6%.

Private Equity

As David Swensen wrote in *Pioneering Portfolio Management*, "In their most basic form, venture and buyout investing represent a riskier means of obtaining equity exposure. The high leverage inherent in buyout transactions and the early-stage nature of venture investing cause investors to experience greater fundamental risk and to expect materially higher investment returns."

Yale has consistently delivered impressive 20%+ returns in private equity for more than the past 30 years. Throughout this book, we will use the term private equity to refer to its two main constituencies, leveraged buyout funds and venture capital funds (or, in shorthand parlance, buyout and venture capital). The endowment benefits from the long-term relationships with the top private equity managers, and its allocation far exceeds the university average. Yale established one of the first private equity programs by allocating capital to a buyout partnership in 1973 and to a venture partnership in 1976. Yale's investment program in private equity is often seen as the gold standard to emulate. Through its underlying managers, Yale was an early investor in Compaq, Oracle, Genentech, Amgen, and Google (where its $300,000 investment grew to $75 million).

Yale focuses on partnerships that focus on a value-added approach to investing, and avoids funds that are sponsored by financial institutions (due to potential conflicts of interest). We take up a much more in-depth examination of private equity in Chapter 5.

In the private equity arena, Yale targets 14.6% returns with 27.7% volatility and virtually no correlation to the rest of the portfolio.

Absolute Return

Yale became the first institutional investor that targeted absolute returns as an asset class in 1990. Yale dedicates half the allocation to event-driven strategies (mergers, spin-offs, bankruptcies), and half to value strategies where securities diverge from their economic value. We examine hedge funds in detail in Chapter 6.

In the absolute return allocation, Yale targets 9.4% returns with 15% volatility and virtually no correlation to the rest of the portfolio.

Summary

- The Yale University endowment has not always been in good shape, and the arrival of David Swensen helped propel Yale into an investment powerhouse.
- Yale generates its exceptional return due to asset allocation and active management.
- Yale seeks wide diversification as an effective means of risk management.
- Most of Yale's portfolio is in equity-like asset classes. Bonds exist only as a hedge against deflation.
- There is a large allocation to real assets and nontraditional asset classes for their return potential and diversifying power.
- Active management is practiced only in the less efficient markets, and Yale generates most of its outperformance in private equity and real assets.
- Yale outperforms its current target Policy Portfolio by over 6% per annum.

Chapter 3

The Harvard Endowment

At the end of the day, Jack's been the single most significant factor in terms of Harvard's strength as an organization, given the billions of dollars he's been able to put on the endowment's books.
                              —MICHAEL HOLLAND, HOLLAND AND CO.

J ack Meyer is to Harvard what David Swensen is to Yale. Although he arrived later (1990), and left earlier (2005), his effect on the Harvard endowment is equally impressive. When he took over the endowment its assets under management were around $5 billion, and by the time he left the portfolio had grown to five times that amount—outperforming the Policy Portfolio and endowment average by about 5% per annum. Figure 3.1 shows the 5- and 10-year annualized returns for the Harvard Management Company (HMC) versus the Policy Portfolio and median institution. Equally as impressive as Yale!

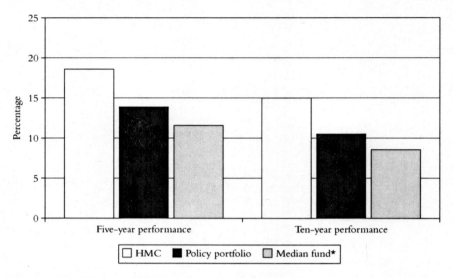

Figure 3.1   Five- and Ten-Year Annualized Average Returns
SOURCE: 2007 Harvard endowment report. Median fund is 19 institutional funds with assets of over
$1 billion, based on information compiled by the Trust Universe Comparison Service (TUCS).

History of the Endowment

Harvard University, which celebrated its 370th anniversary in
2006, is the oldest institution of higher education in the United
States. Founded in 1636, 16 years after the arrival of the Pilgrims at
Plymouth, the university has grown from 9 students with a single
master to an enrollment of more than 18,000 degree candidates. Eight
presidents of the United States—John Adams, John Quincy Adams,
Theodore and Franklin Delano Roosevelt, Rutherford B. Hayes, John
Fitzgerald Kennedy, George W. Bush, and Barack Obama—received
degrees from Harvard. More than 40 Nobel laureates are current or
former faculty members of Harvard.

Harvard was named for its first benefactor, John Harvard of
Charlestown, a young minister who, upon his death in 1638, left his
library and half his estate to the new institution. In 1649, the university received a gift of real estate from members of the Class of 1642

and the Class of 1646. Once a cow yard, this small parcel was dubbed the "Fellows' Orchard" after the alumni planted it with apple trees, and Widener Library now occupies part of the site.

The endowment is now made up of over 11,000 separate funds established over the years to provide scholarships; to maintain libraries, museums, and other collections; to support teaching and research activities; and to provide ongoing support for a wide variety of other activities. Similar to the situation at Yale, the great majority of these funds carry some type of restriction directing that the funds are used for a particular purpose.

The Owner's Mentality

Historically, the Harvard endowment has been structured quite differently from Yale's. While Yale outsources almost all of its fund management to outside managers, Harvard historically has managed most of its money internally, somewhat resembling an in-house hedge fund that, at its peak, had about seven times as many employees looking after its investments (175) as did Yale (around 25).

The early seeds of the modern endowment were planted in the early 1970s. Paul Cabot was the treasurer for 15 years until 1974, and he oversaw growth in the endowment from about $200 million to over $1 billion. He managed the endowment as an account at his firm State Street Management, which was paid a tiny $20,000 fee for doing so. By 1974, the endowment was getting large enough to create a separate structure, and Harvard incorporated its own not-for-profit Harvard Management Company as a wholly owned subsidiary of the university in July of that year. This creation was to the regret of then President Derek Bok, who remarked, "Harvard is an educational institution and has no particular skill in operating an investment company," (*Great Good Fortune: How Harvard Makes Its Money* by Carl Vigeland). Fortunately for Harvard's future students, he would be proven very wrong.

Paul Cabot was followed as treasurer by George Putnam who decided that HMC needed a full-time manager. Putnam promptly hired Walter Cabot, the nephew of Paul Cabot. While much of the capital was managed internally, HMC teamed up with Cambridge Associates to identify some outside managers and ended up allocating about 10% of the portfolio to various firms (none of which were still in place 10 years later). Cabot admitted that he found it difficult to find consistently superior managers. Cabot was one of the early pioneers exploring less efficient markets, and his observations echo the same line of thinking as Swensen's when he joined Yale a number of years later.

The younger Cabot remarked, "I would like to deliver superior results for the account. How can I get them? I don't believe we can pick stocks and bonds in a fashion demonstrably to our benefit. There is too much flow of information out there. I don't think we can achieve our objective through conventional methodologies of picking stocks and bonds. So how do we get to our goal? . . . Endowments are often early in new investment ideas: real estate, venture capital, private deals, and the like. They act like owners, not hired guns, who are more likely to fight for relative performance and thus more likely to get into trouble sooner or later. . . . We have acquired the owner's mentality as against the hired guns mentality."

With respect to Harvard's move into less efficient markets, Cabot remarked, "With this thesis in mind, we look for areas of investment mispricing. We got a notch up through securities lending, which we did very early. The problem with securities lending today is that there are too many people doing it, so they have driven down the margins and taken away most of the profit. Then we were early in the use of derivative products. We noticed that they were being used by the brokerage community in managing its own assets, but not by pensions or endowments. We've now moved into private investing in equities that are unquoted in the marketplace, such as new ventures, leveraged buyouts, oil and gas assets and explorations, and real estate. We've found the pricing less competitive there. We can structure a deal favorably, so the returns are better. Obviously, there is a give-up in liquidity. . . . As to venture capital, we're participants in about sixty limited partnerships" (Train, 1994). Today Harvard allocates its private equity portfolio to over 60 fund groups representing over 150 individual funds and was even the first institutional client of superstar venture capital firm Kleiner Perkins Caufield & Byers.

One could easily use Cabot's comments on securities lending and derivatives to describe the state of private equity today: The problem with private equity today is that *there are too many people doing it, so they have driven down the margins and taken away most of the profit.* This is true of any inefficient asset class when high returns attract attention and an influx of money. The same could be said for any successful business in a capitalistic system.

By the spring of 1987, Harvard had a majority of its endowment in equities but reduced the percentage to about 40% by October. As a result, by the time the October 1987 crash happened, Harvard fell only 13% while the S&P declined around 21%. Cabot was succeeded by Jack Meyer a few years later in 1990.

Harvard's Swensen

After graduating from Denison University, Meyer attended Harvard Business School (where he was the youngest member of the class of 1969). He then worked for 10 years on Wall Street, including stints as a security analyst and investment officer for Lionel Edie and Brown Brothers Harriman & Co. Meyer then became the first chief investment officer for New York City's $20 billion pension fund, and later held a similar job at the then-$2-billion Rockefeller Foundation. Meyer joined HMC in 1990, and the person to recommend his appointment, coincidentally, was none other than Yale's David Swensen.

Meyer introduced the concept of the Policy Portfolio to Harvard when he joined in 1990. Meyer did not feel that Harvard had much of an edge in tactical asset allocation and adhered to the target allocation percentages fairly closely. He felt the true value HMC added was in security selection and relative mispricings among securities rather than market timing. Harvard employed much of this arbitrage style investment strategy in-house where a cheap asset is purchased and an expensive one is simultaneously sold short. Harvard still practices all sorts of arbitrage strategies including merger arbitrage, convertible bond arbitrage, and closed-end fund arbitrage.

Harvard indexes much of its assets in the commodity class and has a large allocation to timber that at times has approached 10% of the entire endowment.

The Special Case of Timber

Harvard was an early pioneer in timber investing and was once the largest institutional timber owner in the world (Harvard even had three lumberjacks on the payroll). Institutions like Harvard have been attracted to timber for its stable return characteristics as well as the noncorrelation to traditional assets and as a nice hedge against inflation.

Forests cover about a third of the total land area in the United States, and of that amount, about half is commercial timberland. Interestingly enough, the United States is the world's largest producer of softwood and hardwood lumber (followed by Canada). Until the 1990s most timber assets were held by large conglomerates that did a poor job of managing the assets effectively. Due to the predictable growth cycle of trees, institutions can buy forests and build a laddered portfolio diversified by tree species, geography, and maturity. Harvard attempts to manage the forests more efficiently, which can include creative uses such as alternative energy generation and the granting of mineral rights. Active investments usually go through brokers called timberland investment management organizations (TIMOs), and they often have multimillion dollar minimums.

It is difficult to benchmark timber returns with an index, but the most widely accepted is the National Council of Real Estate Investment Fiduciaries (NCREIF) Timberland Index. It has been published since 1994 and has returns going back to 1987. The index reports both income and appreciation returns.

The Special Case of Timber (*Continued*)

The index only has two contributors representing more than $3 billion while the TIMO industry has roughly $10 billion worth of timberland. Both this index and other academic studies have shown timber to return around 10%–15% per year with 10%–15% volatility. Most of the total returns from timber investments are due to the biological growth of the trees, while changes in timber prices and land value account for smaller amounts of the total return.

Unfortunately, it is quite difficult for most individual investors to go out and buy a forest, and most timber investments are suited toward private-equity style investing with multiyear lockups and large minimums. Stocks like Plum Creek Timber (PCL), a public REIT that is now the largest nongovernment timber owner in the United States, are freely traded but have the problem of containing stock risk and correlation. The correlation of PCL to the S&P 500 since 1989 is approximately 0.4, and the stock has had historical drawdowns of more than 40%.

The Claymore/Clear Global Timber (CUT) exchange-traded fund (ETF) is the first ETF to launch focusing on the timber area, and it has a global allocation to companies involved in owning and leasing forest land, harvesting timber, selling wood and pulp-based products, and selling paper and packaging materials. The index weights the country allocations by the distribution of forest land across regions of the world. Barclay's quickly followed with the iShares S&P Global Timber & Forestry Index Fund (WOOD) ETF.

While owning a forest is a pure play on the timber industry, owning a stock like PCL or an ETF like CUT or WOOD provides exposure to the management teams and all that goes with running public companies. Some commodity companies partially hedge themselves against price changes in the underlying commodity as well. Many companies are included in stock indexes,

(Continued)

The Special Case of Timber (*Continued*)

which further increases their correlation with stocks. Our belief is that these ETFs will track the forestry and paper products sector more closely than the NCREIF Timberland Index.

Another option would be a closed-end fund that invests directly in timber. There are two of these funds, Cambium Global Timberland (TREE.L) and the Phaunos Timber Fund (PTF.L), but both are traded on the London Stock Exchange (see Chapter 6 for issues surrounding investing in these funds). Both funds charge a management fee (1%–1.5%) as well as a performance fee (20% of returns over 8% annually).

More Money, More Problems

Even though HMC trounced the returns of the average endowment over the course of Meyer's 15 years at the helm, the structure of the endowment management company gained some vocal critics. As a for-profit entity at a nonprofit organization, HMC caused a stir by paying large salaries to some of its employees. These grumblings had been heard since the inception of HMC back in 1974, but as Harvard's endowment approached a massive size, the criticism increased.

Managers earned bonuses based on the amount by which they added value or exceeded the performance of comparable index funds. This is a fairly standard compensation scheme for Wall Street. To discourage excessive risk taking, HMC has employed a "clawback" provision that penalizes a manager who performs spectacularly one year and poorly the next by requiring him to pay back a large portion of his previous bonus.

In 2003, two managers earned over $35 million each. In 2004, HMC paid its top money managers over $100 million total (and about $25 million each to the same top two managers). Meyer himself made $7.2 million in 2004. While overwhelming in some respects, the compensation pales for example when compared to the $5.7 billion gain HMC helped earn in 2007. Such headline grabbing figures eventually tore the structure apart. Many students and alumni had a hard time rationalizing paying these managers multimillion dollar salaries while the university's Nobel Prize-winning professors earned a comparative pittance. The unbiased and logical choice favors keeping the managers in-house.

Meyer remarked that "it was a good deal for Harvard and allowed the school to hang on to top-flight investment talent" (*Boston Globe*, 2004). HMC estimated that the total cost to manage the portfolio internally was 0.5%. Compare that figure to the average hedge fund (2% management fee and 20% of performance), and one can easily see how outsourcing costs Harvard millions, if not billions, in future value. In his recent book *When Markets Collide*, former HMC manager Mohamed El-Erian estimates that it costs HMC twice as much to outsource investment management as opposed to keeping it in-house.

Eventually Meyer had enough of the critics and left Harvard in 2005 to launch his own hedge fund, Convexity Capital Management. Thirty former HMC staffers joined Meyer in what was the largest hedge fund launch to date at $6 billion. Harvard pledged to invest $500 million in the fund, which is somewhat ironic. HMC is now paying Meyer a higher fee to leave Harvard and manage much less of its money. With a 1.25% management fee, Meyer's new firm stands to make $75 million annually—of which $6,250,000 is paid by Harvard—just for turning the lights on. That $75 million is more than 10 times the salary he made at Harvard, and if Convexity performs well, the sky is the limit with a 20% performance fee.

So far Meyer is the sixth direct spin-off from HMC. Other former employees who left HMC to start their own funds include Jonathan Jacobson who started Highfields Capital Management and Jeffrey Larson who started Sowood Capital. HMC often invests in these spin-offs, and unfortunately for Harvard its $500 million investment in Sowood lost $350 million when the hedge fund experienced major losses in 2007. For Yale's part, Swensen's protégées interestingly often end up at other endowments and foundations including those of Princeton, Carnegie Mellon, MIT, and Bowdoin.

When Meyer first arrived at Harvard, only 20% of the endowment was managed externally, mostly in the real estate, private equity, and timber areas. Meyer left in 2005, and now most of the funds are managed externally similar to the Yale model. HMC had only had two CIOs for the first 30 years of its existence, and then two new ones in the next few years. After Meyer's departure, Harvard landed the superstar emerging markets bond manager Mohamed El-Erian from West Coast-based PIMCO, where he managed over $30 billion of PIMCO's $500 billion in assets. El-Erian only stuck around for two years before returning to Southern California to join Bill Gross at the now $800 billion PIMCO as co-CEO and co-CIO. Just recently, Jane Mendillo was appointed president and CIO of HMC. Mendillo worked at Harvard previously and oversaw a portfolio of $7 billion, roughly a third of the endowment at the time. She had served as the CIO at Wellesley College since 2002. Hopefully (from Harvard's standpoint) she stays longer than two years.

How Harvard Does It

The most powerful tool an investor has working for him or her is diversification. True diversification allows you to build portfolios with higher returns for the same risk. Most investors, institutional and individual, are far less diversified than they should be. They're way over-committed to U.S. stocks and marketable securities.
—JACK MEYER, SMART MONEY, 2007

Table 3.1 shows that while historically investing about 60% in stocks, 30% in bonds, and 10% in cash, Harvard began a push into alternative strategies in the late 1970s before going full steam into private equity and real assets in the late 1980s and early 1990s. While Yale only breaks its asset allocation into 7 categories, Harvard breaks its allocation into 12.

Like Yale, Harvard beats its benchmark in every single asset class. Also like Yale, Harvard outperforms the benchmark most significantly in the private equity category, where Harvard has delivered a whopping 16.6% excess returns per year. More interesting is the edge that Harvard has developed in the notoriously efficient bond markets. HMC outperformed the benchmark by substantial amounts in both domestic and foreign fixed income (even more than in equities). All told, Harvard outperformed its benchmark by over 4% per annum. See Table 3.2.

Table 3.1   Policy Portfolio

	1980	1991	1996	2000	2007	2008
Equities:						
Domestic equities	66%	40%	36%	22%	12%	12%
Developed foreign equities		18	15	15	11	12
Emerging markets equities			9	9	8	10
Private Equities		12	15	15	13	11
Total equities	**66**	**70**	**75**	**61**	**44**	**45**
Fixed-income:						
Domestic bonds	27	15	13	10	7	5
Foreign bonds	8	5	5	4	3	3
High-yield bonds		2	2	3	3	1
Total fixed-income	**35**	**22**	**20**	**17**	**13**	**9**
Real assets:						
Commodities	0	6	3	6	16	17
Real estate	0	7	7	7	10	9
Inflation-indexed bonds	0	0	0	7	5	7
Total real assets	**0**	**13**	**10**	**20**	**31**	**33**
Absolute return and special situations	0	0	0	5	17	18
Cash	−1	−5	−5	−3	−5	−5
TOTAL	**100%**	**100%**	**100%**	**100%**	**100%**	**100%**

Source: 2007 Harvard endowment report.

Harvard's AAA credit rating allows it to borrow cheaply and to implement strategies other investment managers cannot. No wonder El-Erian highlighted that one of the areas of value that HMC adds to the portfolio is in risk management. He stated:

> It's getting very crowded, not only in terms of asset allocations, but in terms of finding the right implementation vehicles. There's a limit to how much superior investment expertise is out there. So the asset allocation is going to be less potent

Table 3.2 Asset Class Performance

	5-Year Performance (Annualized)			10-Year Performance (Annualized)		
	HMC	Benchmark	Relative	HMC	Benchmark	Relative
Equities						
Domestic equities	13.1%	11.3%	1.9%	11.6%	8.4%	3.2%
Foreign equities	19.8	18.5	1.3	11.3	8.4	2.9
Emerging equities	32.0	30.9	1.1	14.6	13.7	0.9
Private equities	20.0	16.4	3.6	30.6	14.0	16.6
Fixed-income						
Domestic bonds	14.5	5.2	9.3	13.7	6.8	6.9
Foreign bonds	16.9	6.8	10.1	13.3	4.9	8.4
High-yield	18.1	13.8	4.3	9.8	4.9	4.9
Real assets						
Commodities	17.4	9.2	8.2	12.4	6.2	6.1
Real estate	21.1	15.7	5.4	17.3	15.1	2.2
Inflation bonds	6.2	6.3	0	NA	NA	
Absolute returns	15.0	11.0	4.0	NA	NA	
TOTAL	**18.4%**	**13.8%***	**4.7%**	**15%**	**10.5%***	**4.4%**
Median fund		11.6%**			8.4%**	

Source: HMC web site.
* Policy Portfolio
** Large fund mean and median performance as measured by Trust Universe Comparison Service (TUCS).

52

because there are more people doing it. And then the global liquidity situation is changing as well. So our view is that performance in the future needs something more—two things more: first, better risk management, because correlated risk has become a big issue, and diversified asset allocation no longer gives you the risk mitigating characteristics it used to. Second, is identifying new secular themes that will play out over the next five years, and trying to be a first mover in those, and that's what we're working very hard at doing. (*Pensions and Investments Magazine*, 2007)

Summary

- The Harvard endowment is the largest in the world.
- The seeds of an unconventional portfolio were planted in the 1970s and 1980s.
- Like Yale, Harvard seeks wide diversification, and focuses on equity-like asset classes.
- Real assets and alternatives have a large allocation in the portfolio. Timber investments, which provide stable, less correlated returns, is an area where Harvard has developed an expertise.
- Harvard has had very strong returns, outperforming its peers and the asset class benchmarks.
- Harvard has outperformed the target Policy Portfolio by over 5% per annum.
- Once run like an internal hedge fund, Harvard is morphing into the Yale style of outsourcing its endowment management.

Chapter 4

Building Your Own Ivy League Portfolio

"It would be like advising my son or daughter to drop out of school to play basketball with the goal of becoming the next Michael Jordan."
—MOHAMED EL-ERIAN

That is the response the former manager of the Harvard endowment used when asked this question, "Can an individual investor hope to replicate the fantastic results of the top endowments?" That's harsh, but you have to be an empirical skeptic when it comes to financial markets commentary. In this chapter we set out to examine the possibilities anyway. If an investor can't replicate the results of the top endowments, why not? Is it due to active or passive management? Or maybe it is due to the allocations to private equity and hedge funds? How much will the investor underperform against the endowments? Can he or she even come close?

We believe that the individual investor can replicate many of the investment strategies of the top endowments, and by doing so can achieve increased risk-adjusted returns. This chapter examines how an investor can construct a Policy Portfolio to mimic the Super Endowments using exchange-traded funds (ETFs). We back test the hypothetical allocation to examine the historical performance relative to the Harvard and Yale endowments. Practical implementation issues including indexing, taxes, discipline, and rebalancing are examined to come up with the optimal approach.

Do as I Do—Shadowing the Super Endowments

The previous two chapters focused on the outstanding returns of the Yale and Harvard endowments. While Yale has slightly outperformed Harvard, the two returns streams are quite similar. Since 1985, Yale has about a 1.4% performance edge over Harvard, with slightly higher volatility. The returns of the two endowments are highly correlated (over .90), suggesting that the management teams may construct similar portfolios using comparable strategies. See Table 4.1.

Returns of 15%–16% with 10% volatility and a Sharpe Ratio over 1.0 put these endowments in rarefied air. During the period depicted in Table 4.1, Harvard only had two down years and Yale only one.

Table 4.2 shows the year-by-year results of the Harvard and Yale endowments averaged, along with five major asset classes and their investable indexes—U.S. stocks (S&P 500), foreign stocks (MSCI EAFE), 10-year U.S. government bonds, real estate (FTSE NAREIT Index), and commodities (GSCI). (While there are only three mega asset classes—stocks, bonds, and real assets—we break it out into five in this chapter.) The most problematic of the five asset classes to index is the real estate asset class. Real estate investment trusts (REITs) are not a direct proxy for real estate and combine features of both equity and fixed income. Because there have not been any alternative investable indexes historically, we use the REIT index here.[1]

On average, the endowments outperformed any one asset class by 3% to 7% per year with a lot less volatility. The worst years for Harvard and Yale were −2.7% and −0.2%, respectively—pedestrian compared to the −17.99% experienced by the S&P 500 in 2002 and the stunning drawdowns of 2008 (and calendar year returns were even worse).

---

[1] There are currently a number of housing and real estate indexes being developed into investable products. These may be better proxies for the real estate asset class than the current REITs.

Table 4.1 Annual Returns of the Harvard and Yale Endowments (1985–2008), Fiscal Year Ending June 30

	Harvard	Yale
1985	26.8%	25.8%
1986	31.3	36.0
1987	19.9	22.8
1988	5.7	−0.2
1989	12.8	17.3
1990	7.5	13.1
1991	1.1	2.0
1992	11.8	13.2
1993	16.7	17.3
1994	9.8	12.0
1995	16.8	15.7
1996	26.0	25.7
1997	25.8	21.8
1998	20.5	18.0
1999	12.2	12.2
2000	32.2	41.0
2001	−2.7	9.2
2002	−0.5	0.7
2003	12.5	8.8
2004	21.1	19.4
2005	19.2	22.3
2006	16.7	22.9
2007	23.0	28.0
2008	8.6	4.5
Annualized Return	15.23%	16.62%
Volatility	9.55%	10.40%
Sharpe (5%)	1.07	1.12
Best Year	32.2%	41.0%
Worst Year	−2.7%	−0.2%
Correlation to Harvard	—	0.91
Correlation to Yale	0.91	—

Source: Yale and Harvard endowment reports.

Table 4.2 Annual Returns of the Harvard and Yale Endowments vs. Five Major Asset Classes (1985–2008), Fiscal Year Ending June 30th

	Harvard and Yale (average)	U.S. Stocks	Foreign Stocks	U.S. Govt Bonds	Real Estate	Commodities
1985	26.30%	30.96%	23.74%	42.35%	30.05%	−6.58%
1986	33.65	35.82	89.60	34.13	7.94	3.79
1987	21.35	25.16	58.73	0.11	8.01	34.99
1988	2.75	−6.91	4.32	5.84	−2.12	12.06
1989	15.05	20.57	9.79	15.07	1.69	36.26
1990	10.30	16.49	3.53	6.11	−11.19	13.42
1991	1.55	7.40	−11.23	10.09	10.46	27.03
1992	12.50	13.41	−0.31	16.59	11.70	6.64
1993	17.00	13.63	20.70	17.65	25.83	−5.92
1994	10.90	1.41	17.30	−5.06	6.20	0.35
1995	16.25	26.07	1.95	16.79	4.75	−5.51
1996	25.85	26.00	13.62	2.39	17.60	44.83
1997	23.80	34.70	13.16	8.55	34.27	1.14
1998	19.25	30.16	6.38	14.72	6.39	−22.76
1999	12.20	22.76	7.92	2.33	−10.18	−7.74
2000	36.60	7.25	17.44	4.63	0.74	59.63
2001	3.25	−14.83	−23.32	10.49	25.35	−4.02
2002	0.10	−17.99	−9.22	9.58	17.37	−8.31
2003	10.65	0.25	−6.06	15.03	5.81	24.09
2004	20.25	19.11	32.85	−3.93	26.61	26.19
2005	20.75	6.32	14.13	9.88	30.08	21.22
2006	19.80	8.63	27.07	4.52	16.36	13.42
2007	25.50	20.59	27.47	5.77	10.88	−13.18
2008	6.55	−13.12	−10.15	12.76	−16.55	75.99
Annualized Return	15.95%	11.98%	11.66%	9.81%	9.94%	11.35%
Volatility	9.75%	15.60%	23.60%	11.00%	13.58%	24.12%
Sharpe (5%)	1.12	0.45	0.28	0.44	0.36	0.26
Best Year	36.60%	35.82%	89.60%	42.35%	34.27%	59.62%
Worst Year	0.10%	−17.99%	−23.32%	−5.06%	−11.19%	−22.76%

Table 4.2 Annual Returns of the Harvard and Yale Endowments vs. Five Major Asset Classes (1985–2008), Fiscal Year Ending June 30th (*Continued*)

	Harvard and Yale (average)	U.S. Stocks	Foreign Stocks	U.S. Govt Bonds	Real Estate	Commodities
Correlation to H + Y	—	0.70	0.71	0.19	0.25	0.09
Maximum Drawdown	—	−44.73%	−47.47%	−11.64%	−28.24%	−48.25%

Source: Harvard and Yale endowment reports. U.S. stocks: S&P 500; Foreign stocks: MSCI EAFE; Commodities: GSCI; Real Estate: REITs; Bonds: 10-year U.S. government.

The average return stream for the Super Endowments is largely correlated with equity returns, both domestic and foreign (around 0.7), which makes sense given their bias to equity-like investments. The endowments have less correlation to the other asset classes. Many of the asset classes in Table 4.2 had painfully large drawdowns. Most investors do not notice upside volatility as much as they do downside volatility, drawdowns, and actually losing money.

Maximum drawdown simply measures the peak to valley loss in an investment. To illustrate, if you bought stock in a company when it was $100 and it drifted down to $75 before eventually going up to $200, you would have at one point had a 25% drawdown ($100 to $75).

Figure 4.1 is a chart of the S&P 500 over this time period (1985–2008), and Figure 4.2 is a chart of the resulting drawdowns. While there

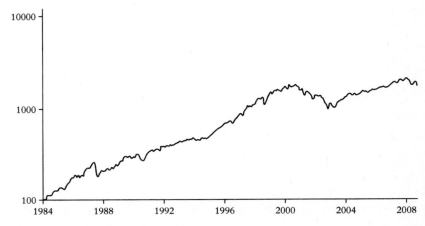

Figure 4.1 S&P 500 from 1985 to 2008

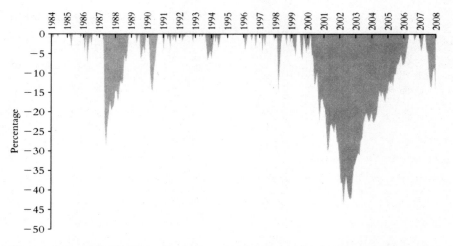

Figure 4.2   S&P 500 Drawdowns from 1984 to 2008, Fiscal Year Ending June 30th

have been many smaller drawdowns of 5% to 10%, an investor can painfully remember the greater than 40% drawdown in the 2000–2003 bear market. The sharp 1987 crash is the second biggest drawdown over the time period, but the market recovered quickly and was hitting new highs again less than two years later. The most recent illustration is the greater than 40% drawdown that the S&P 500 experienced in 2008 (not shown).

Because the endowments only report annual returns, it is hard to estimate the drawdown figure over this time period, but 30% is a reasonable estimate. We will take up the topic of drawdowns again and how to best avoid them in Chapter 7.

For simplicity and because it is difficult for the individual investor to access hedge funds and private equity (discussed in more detail in Chapters 5 and 6), Table 4.3 removes those allocations (and cash allocation) to determine what a portfolio would look like without them ("normalized").

What would the historical returns of this portfolio look like? Because some of the asset classes did not exist during the entire 1985–2008 time period, we grouped the percentages into five main asset classes to obtain historical performance. We are just looking for ballpark numbers, and the main asset classes should work to give a good overall picture.

We included emerging stocks with foreign developed stocks because they did not exist as an investable index for most of the period.

Table 4.3 Policy Portfolios of Harvard and Yale Endowments vs. S&P 500, 1985–2008

	Harvard 2007	Yale 2007	Averaged	Harvard Normalized	Yale Normalized	Averaged
Domestic Stocks	12.00%	11.00%	11.50%	15.79%	18.97%	17.38%
Foreign Developed Stocks	12.00	6.00	9.00	15.79	10.34	13.07
Foreign Emerging Stocks	10.00	9.00	9.50	13.16	15.52	14.34
Bonds	9.00	4.00	6.50	11.74	6.90	9.37
TIPS	7.00	0.00	3.50	9.21	0.00	4.61
Real Estate	9.00	14.00	11.50	11.84	24.14	17.99
Commodities	17.00	14.00	15.50	22.37	24.14	23.25
Private Equity	11.00	19.00	15.00	—	—	—
Hedge Funds	18.00	23.00	20.50	—	—	—
Cash	−5.00	0.00	−2.50	—	—	—
Total	100%	100%	100%	100%	100%	100%

Source: Harvard and Yale endowment reports.

Likewise, Treasury Inflation-Protected Securities, or TIPS, did not exist until 1997 in the United States. They have since surged to over 15% of the U.S. Treasury market.[2] TIPS are a little problematic to categorize as they are real assets that do not correlate much with anything, but synthetic data series reveal that they have the most correlation with commodities and bonds (but still low around .2 to .3).

We lump TIPS in with the bond category, and given that TIPS did not exist until 1997 and they have a small weighting at 5%, their inclusion should not make that much of a difference in total portfolio performance statistics. In Table 4.4, we compare the Harvard and Yale allocations to our own simplified allocation.

---

[2]In countries with longer issuance histories like the United Kingdom, inflation-indexed bonds account for nearly half of government debt.

Table 4.4   Harvard and Yale Endowment Allocations

Asset Class	Simple	Harvard and Yale
Domestic Stocks	20%	18%
Foreign Stocks	30	27
Bonds	15	14
Real Estate	15	18
Commodities	20	23
Total	100%	100%

Table 4.5   The Ivy Portfolio

The Ivy Portfolio	Simple
Domestic Stocks	20%
Foreign Stocks	20
Bonds	20
Real Estate	20
Commodities	20
Total	100%

Because we like things as simple as possible, we rounded out the allocation even further (the two allocations should be nearly identical in performance) in Table 4.5.

The result is an even 20% allocation to the five asset classes. We call this portfolio the Ivy Portfolio as it is very simple but still reflects the general allocations of the top endowments without hedge funds and private equity. Namely, a preference toward equity assets, real assets to protect against inflation, and a small bond allocation to insure against deflation risk. (We expand the Ivy Portfolio later to include more granular asset classes, but this exercise is mainly to approximate historical performance.)

Table 4.6 shows the returns to a portfolio divided evenly among the five asset classes at 20% each, as well as the classic 60%/40% stocks and bonds split. Both portfolios are rebalanced yearly.

Table 4.6   Returns of the Harvard and Yale Endowments vs. Two Portfolios (1985–2008), Fiscal Year Ending June 30th

	Harvard and Yale (average)	60% Stocks 40% Bonds	Ivy Portfolio
1985	26.30%	35.52%	24.10%
1986	33.65	35.14	34.25
1987	21.35	15.14	25.40
1988	2.75	−1.81	2.64
1989	15.05	18.37	16.68
1990	10.30	12.34	5.67
1991	1.55	8.47	8.75
1992	12.50	14.68	9.61
1993	17.00	15.24	14.38
1994	10.90	−1.18	4.04
1995	16.25	22.36	8.81
1996	25.85	16.56	20.89
1997	23.80	24.24	18.37
1998	19.25	23.99	6.98
1999	12.20	14.59	3.02
2000	36.60	6.20	17.93
2001	3.25	−4.70	−1.27
2002	0.10	−6.96	−1.71
2003	10.65	6.16	7.83
2004	20.25	9.89	20.17
2005	20.75	7.75	16.33
2006	19.80	3.37	12.19
2007	25.50	14.66	10.31
2008	6.55	−2.76	9.79
Annualized Return	15.95%	11.42%	11.97%
Volatility	9.75%	11.40%	8.85%
Sharpe (5%)	1.12	0.56	0.79
Best Year	36.60%	35.52%	34.25%
Worst Year	0.10%	−6.96%	−1.71%
Correlation to H + Y	—	0.65	0.80

Source: Harvard and Yale endowment annual reports.

The returns of both the 60/40 portfolio and the Ivy Portfolio are fairly highly correlated to the returns of the Super Endowments. This makes sense because both portfolios consist largely of equity risk.

The Ivy Portfolio has much higher risk-adjusted returns than the 60/40 mix and is more correlated to the Super Endowments, likely due to the allocation to real assets. For similar levels of volatility the Super Endowments outperform the passive portfolios by over 4% per year. (And for the past 10 years the endowment edge has been closer to 8% per annum.) A significant amount of that outperformance comes from the private equity portfolio. A case could be made that the endowments have artificially smoothed volatility due to the private equity investments (private equity investments tend to get marked to market less frequently), but the results should be very similar.

A return to volatility ratio of about 1:1 (or a little better) is about the best an investor can hope to do for a passive portfolio without exposure to alternatives. But that's not bad! The Ivy Portfolio even outperforms the target performance of the Yale Policy Portfolio, which aims for about 10% returns with 12% volatility.

Doing as the endowments do leads to a well-balanced portfolio, especially on a risk-adjusted basis. What exactly does that mean?

Risk-Adjusted Returns

The Sharpe Ratio is a measure of the risk-adjusted return of an investment. While there are a lot of ways to measure risk, the Sharpe Ratio uses the volatility of an investment. Originally developed by Stanford Professor William Sharpe, it is simply the return of an investment (R) minus cash sitting in T-bills (otherwise known as the risk-free rate, Rf), divided by the volatility of the investment (σ). Cash will have a Sharpe Ratio of zero.

$$S = (R - Rf)/\sigma$$

A good rule of thumb for Sharpe Ratios is that asset classes, over the long term, have Sharpes around 0.2 to 0.3. A "dummy" 60/40 allocation to stocks/bonds is around .4. The Ivy Portfolio allocation is around 0.6. However, over shorter periods, the numbers can bounce all

Table 4.7 Returns of Famous Investors (1986–1999)

1986–1999	Windsor	Berkshire	Quantum	Tiger	Ford
Return	13.83%	24.99%	21.94%	17.54%	14.43%
Sharpe	0.62	0.64	1.02	1.06	0.96

1986–1999	Harvard	S&P 500	U.S. Treasury	U.S. T-bills	U.S. Inflation
Return	15.17%	18.04%	7.78%	5.39%	3.13%
Sharpe	1.15	0.98	0.36	0.00	−1.67

Source: *Scenarios for Risk Management and Global Investment Strategies* by William T. Ziemba. Published by John Wiley & Sons, 2008.

Vanguard Windsor Fund—Managed by John Neff for 30 years, this fund was regularly in the top 5% of all mutual funds.

Berkshire Hathaway—Warren Buffett's conglomerate holding company has returned over 20% for the past 40 years.

Quantum Fund—George Soros comanaged this fund with Jim Rogers, and it returned over 40% a year in the 1970s. From 1969 to 2001 he did over 30% per year.

Tiger Management—Managed by Julian Robertson.

The Ford Foundation—One of the top performing foundations.

over the place. From 1900–2008, the S&P 500 has had Sharpe Ratios per decade ranging from −.08 (the 1970s) to 1.4 (the 1950s).

One of the problems with the Sharpe Ratio is that it penalizes upside volatility. An investor likes volatility to the upside (making money), but dislikes volatility to the downside (losing money). Table 4.7 shows returns from the book *Scenarios for Risk Management and Global Investment Strategies* by Rachel and William T. Ziemba. It contains some of the most famous and successful investors of all time.

The first observation is how outstanding the returns were for stocks in this period, which inflates the Sharpe Ratio for the S&P 500 to one of the highest levels it has seen in the past century. The second observation is that many of these successful managers are getting penalized for making money with their upside volatility.

To gain a full understanding of a manager's performance, investors should use alternative metrics to evaluate managers, but in the interest of avoiding complexity (and because most investors are familiar with the Sharpe Ratio), that is the metric we will use throughout the book. Some alternative metrics include:

- **Sortino Ratio:** uses only the volatility of negative asset returns in the denominator (similar to Ziemba's downside symmetric Sharpe Ratio).

- **Sterling Ratio:** uses the average maximum drawdown in the denominator.
- **MAR (or Calmar) Ratio:** uses maximum drawdown in the denominator.
- **Ulcer Index:** Measures the length and severity of drawdowns (one of our favorites).

The average return and volatility can tell you a lot, but if you really want to get deeper in the subject check out the third and fourth moments of the return distribution, skew and kurtosis. Nonlinear strategies like option selling can artificially inflate the Sharpe Ratio as they have incredibly consistent good performance until they don't (which is usually a huge or total blowup like the infamous case of Long-Term Capital Management).

The Ivy Portfolio is a well diversified "all-weather" portfolio that should hold up in various economic environments.

Do as I Say

Although we have derived the Ivy Portfolio from the Harvard and Yale annual reports, why not compare these allocations with the allocations the endowment managers themselves suggested in their books? Let's see if there is any difference in "do as I do" and "do as I say."

Both Mohamed El-Erian (*When Markets Collide*) and David Swensen (*Unconventional Success*) recommended portfolios for the individual investor in their books. Table 4.8 is El-Erian's recommended portfolio.

This allocation is expected to return 5% to 7% after inflation with volatility of 8% to12%. Those numbers are in-line with the historical Ivy Portfolio returns as well as the Yale Policy Portfolio expected returns. El-Erian defines special opportunities as "investment opportunities that are attractive but do not fit comfortably into the categories I have covered so far . . . they usually relate to two types of activities: new longer-term activities that are supported by a secular hypothesis but are yet to gain broad-based acceptance; and shorter-term activities that materialize due to sharp dislocations that involve significant

Table 4.8 El-Erian Allocation

	Allocation (%)
U.S. Stocks	15
Foreign Developed Stocks	15
Emerging Market Stocks	12
Private	7
U.S. Government Bonds	5
International Bonds	9
Real Estate	6
Commodities	11
TIPS	5
Infrastructure	5
Special Opportunities	8

Table 4.9 Various Allocations without Alternatives

	Harvard and Yale (average)	El-Erian (no alt)	Swensen (no alt)
Domestic Stocks	17.29%	18.07%	30.00%
Foreign Developed Stocks	13.53	18.07	15.00
Foreign Emerging Stocks	14.29	14.46	5.00
U.S. Bonds	6.77	6.02	15.00
International Bonds	2.26	10.84	—
TIPS	5.26	6.02	15.00
Real Estate	17.29	13.25	20.00
Commodities	23.31	13.25	—
Total	**100.00%**	**100.00%**	**100.00%**

overshoots." El-Erian has a slightly more complicated portfolio, and to compare apples-to-apples we removed the private equity allocation, the special situations allocation, and we lumped the 5% infrastructure allocation in with real estate. (And because the portfolio only adds up to 98% for some odd reason, we allocated 2% to cash.) Table 4.9 shows both the allocations versus the Harvard and Yale allocation.

El-Erian comes pretty close to the endowment allocation, albeit with more in foreign bonds and less in real estate and commodities (which is likely influenced by his expertise in managing foreign bonds at PIMCO). Swensen has the outlier portfolio with more in U.S. stocks, and curiously, more in U.S. bonds and nothing in commodities. It is strange that Swensen did not recommend commodities in either of his books, although he possibly felt that TIPS would better approximate inflation protection than would commodities. Swensen has a new edition of his book *Pioneering Portfolio Management* due in 2009 and hopefully he will take up the topic of commodity investing in it.

TIPS act as a good hedge against inflation and unexpected inflation, and they have a fixed coupon rate that is lower than Treasury bonds of similar maturity. However with TIPS the principal amount of the bonds is adjusted upward every six months based on changes in the consumer price index (CPI), a proxy for inflation. If the United States experiences deflation, the principal cannot decline below par at maturity. TIPS are best held in a tax-exempt account as the coupon and principal increase are taxable.

If you further simplify these allocations by lumping TIPS in with real assets (problematic as we mentioned before), and then rounding the allocations, you get four very similar allocations, as shown in Table 4.10.

The biggest difference between these portfolios and most individual investor portfolios is that the endowment managers have a significant amount in real assets. Why are the endowments making such a big bet on real assets?

Inflation Is the Enemy

If you recall, the endowment's worst enemy is inflation. Table 4.11 shows asset class returns divided into two periods of rising interest rates

Table 4.10 Various Allocations without Alternatives

	Harvard and Yale (average)	Ivy	El-Erian	Swensen
Stocks	50%	40%	50%	50%
Bonds	10	20	20	15
Real Assets	40	40	30	35
Total	**100%**	**100%**	**100%**	**100%**

Table 4.11   Returns of Asset Classes during Periods of High and Low Inflation, 1972–2007

	U.S. Stocks	Foreign Stocks	U.S. Bonds	Commodities	Real Estate	Inflation
High Inflation	8.46%	12.54%	3.27%	19.16%	11.16%	8.70%
Low Inflation	14.11%	14.24%	10.84%	12.65%	12.83%	3.15%

and high inflation (1972–1981), and falling interest rates and low inflation (1982–2007). As you can see, commodities perform much better in inflationary environments, therefore providing a hedge during these periods.

In periods of low inflation and declining interest rates, stocks, foreign stocks, bonds, and REITs all performed better, which makes intuitive sense because they are all capital assets. Investors derive the value of stocks and bonds by discounting their current and expected future cash flows by their cost of capital. For stocks these cash flows are current and future earnings, for bonds, they are future coupon and principal payments. In periods of low inflation, and thus low interest rates, the cost of capital is low, which results in higher cash flows for investors, for which they are willing to pay higher valuations. (Note: For the majority of the history of the United States the dollar was on a precious metal exchange rate, and there was very little inflation.)

Historical returns of commodity indexes have been in-line with stocks with similar volatility, but because commodities are real assets (i.e., corn, gold, oil), they have different sources of return than stocks and bonds. Some commodities are consumable (soybeans), some are used as economic inputs (copper), while others are stores of value (gold). Unlike companies and bondholders whose cash flows are eroded by inflation, commodities benefit from higher prices in inflationary periods.

Many investors have a hard time getting comfortable with the idea of allocating a portion of their portfolio to commodities. That behavior is somewhat ironic as most investors have much more daily interaction with commodities than they do with stocks and bonds.

The best review of commodities' role in a portfolio is the white paper by Ibbotson Associates (commissioned by PIMCO) titled, "Strategic Asset Allocation and Commodities." As usual, we will link to this paper (and many other important papers on commodities) on the Ivy Portfolio web site. How much to include in the portfolio? The Ibbotson study suggests a significant amount.

Bob Greer of PIMCO suggests that "Ibbotson projected future commodity returns using three different methods: the capital asset pricing model (CAPM), the building-blocks method and a combination of the first two methods. The optimal allocation to commodities varied depending on the method. At the 10% standard deviation level—a moderate risk level similar to a standard portfolio of 60% stocks and 40% bonds—the optimal allocation to commodities ranged from about 22% using the capital asset pricing model to as large as 28.9% using the building-blocks method. Even at the conservative 5% risk level, optimal allocations to commodities were relatively large, ranging from about 9% up to nearly 14%. Regardless of the method used in projecting future commodity returns, portfolios that included commodities in the opportunity set were also more efficient than those that excluded commodities, based on the Sharpe Ratio." (PIMCO web site)

Readers of our blog World Beta[3] are aware that we are proponents of investing in commodities, and El-Erian recommends them as well: "Commodities also serve as great diversifiers, and they provide some downside protection against a geo-political shock emanating from the Middle East. A good idea is to purchase a diversified commodities mutual fund or an ETF (exchange-traded commodities fund)." (*Fortune*, 2007.)

Managed futures (at least the trend-following ones, which are the vast majority of the Commodity Trading Advisors, or CTAs) are nothing more than a tactical long/short approach to one asset class, which happens to be commodities (and sometimes other futures contracts including interest rates and financials). Don't get confused; we'll take that topic up in Chapter 7.

---

[3]www.mebanefaber.com

Now that we have taken a look at what the endowments do, as well as what they say, how does an investor go about implementing their recommendations in a portfolio?

Creating an All-Weather Policy Portfolio through Indexing

Jack Meyer gives this advice to the individual investor in a 2004 *BusinessWeek* interview: "First, get diversified. Come up with a portfolio that covers a lot of asset classes. Second, you want to keep your fees low. That means avoiding the most hyped but expensive funds, in favor of low-cost index funds. And finally, invest for the long term. Investors should simply have index funds to keep their fees low and their taxes down." (Symonds, 2004)

In short: diversify, avoid fees and taxes, index, and take a long-term view. This section details how to construct a Policy Portfolio based on the Ivy Portfolio allocation.

We've already tackled diversification by investing in numerous uncorrelated asset classes. Avoiding fees by indexing is the simplest and best way to gain access to an asset class or passive beta. Indexing allows the investor to hold the entire market with few expenses or advisory fees, low turnover, and high tax efficiency. Index funds were first launched in the 1970s in response to the expense-ridden underperformance of active managers.[4]

The percentage of active funds that beat their benchmark index is pretty slim indeed. David Swensen agrees. "A miniscule 4% of funds produce market-beating after-tax results with a scant 0.6% (annual) margin of gain. The 96% of funds that fail to meet or beat the Vanguard 500 Index Fund lose by a wealth-destroying margin of 4.8% per annum." (Bogle, 2007)

---

[4]If you are not convinced of the importance of indexing, pick up a copy of *The Little Book of Common Sense Investing* by Vanguard founder Jack Bogle. Bogle estimates the all-in costs of equity mutual funds at around 3% to 3.5% a year. (Expense ratio (1.5%) + portfolio turnover (1%) + sales charges (.5%)). Add on the poor timing of individual investors, and over the past 25 years they have underperformed the indexes by 5% per annum!

Why is it so hard to beat the indexes? There are a number of reasons, but below we examine one that is not talked about (or studied) often. People assume that long-term returns of individual stocks adhere to a normal distribution. This has simply not been the case.[5] For every Microsoft there were hundreds of below average software companies. For every Exxon there were hundreds of below average oil & gas companies. For every Wells Fargo there were hundreds of below average financial services companies. Capitalism has resulted in a small group of enormous winners, a majority of slightly below average performers, and a substantial number of complete failures.

To illustrate why indexing is hard to beat, see Figure 4.3 from Eric Crittenden and Cole Wilcox at Blackstar Funds[6] who examined all stocks in the Russell 3000 since 1983. The Russell 3000 Index measures the performance of the largest 3000 U.S. companies representing approximately 98% of the investable U.S. equity market.

About 40% of stocks had a negative return over their lifetime, and about 20% of stocks lost nearly all of their value. A little more than 10% of stocks recorded huge wins over 500%.

Eric Crittenden, the portfolio manager at Blackstar observes, "Our interpretation of these findings is to conclude that the stock market is simply an extension of what we see every day in business. A small minority of businesses are well run and blessed with successful ideas. Some businesses are modestly profitable. Many businesses struggle to break even and a large percentage end up being failures. To us it seems the 80/20 rule applies to the stock market: 80% of the gains are a function of 20% of the stocks."

Remember, the majority of this time frame includes one of the biggest bull markets in history.

What about comparing the stocks with their underlying index? Figure 4.4 is a chart of the annualized returns of individual stocks versus the annualized returns of the Russell 3000 index. The chart shows the results of subtracting the Russell 3000 annualized return from each individual stock's annualized return during its lifetime.

---

[5]Plenty of discussion in the book, *The Black Swan* by Nassim Taleb.
[6]Their research, including a great white paper titled "Does Trendfollowing Work on Stocks," can be found on their site, www.blackstarfunds.com.

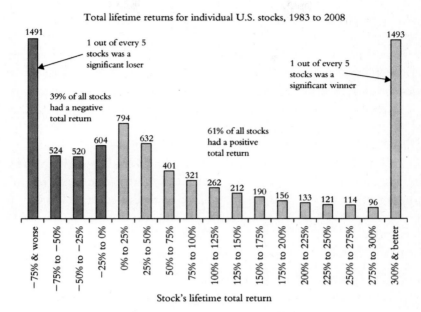

Figure 4.3 Total Returns for U.S. Stocks (1983–2008)
SOURCE: Blackstar Funds.

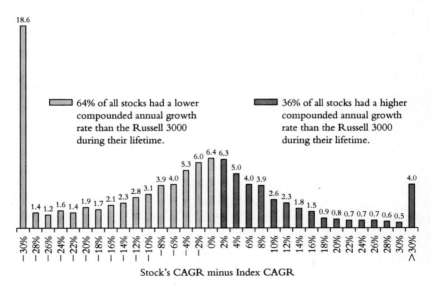

Figure 4.4 Relative Compounded Annual Growth Rate of Individual Stocks vs. Russell 3000.

The takeaway is that 64% of all stocks underperformed the Russell 3000 index during their lifetime and 36% of all stocks outperformed the Russell 3000 index during their lifetime. If most stocks are underperforming the index in which they are members, then a relatively few stocks must be responsible for a majority of the gains.

There are more conclusions one can draw from these studies, and the first is the efficacy of momentum. There has probably been more academic literature on the effectiveness of momentum as a factor in stock and asset class returns than any other factor. One of the most famous models in finance, the Fama French Factor model, includes momentum as the most predictive factor of future returns. We take up this topic in Chapter 7, and Appendix A includes a brief review of the literature.[7]

In the end, it is important to keep in mind that:

- Capitalism is a dynamic process, and many businesses fail.
- Observing the long-term total returns for all stocks shows a very non-normal distribution that consists of a small minority of huge winners, a majority of below average performers, and a significant number of complete failures.
- If you are going to pick stocks, realize that the blind odds of picking a winner more accurately than the index are against you.
- Almost half of stocks have a negative rate of return over their lifetimes, and one in five loses almost all of its value.
- Indexing is the best way to ensure that you will own the big winners.
- Momentum works.

Implementing Your Portfolio

Now that we have talked about how well indexing works, how should the individual investor implement the portfolio? We are agnostic as to what structure to use—be it with mutual funds, ETFs, swaps, or futures. Depending on the individual or institution, different structures make more sense. For the most part, a simple portfolio of low-cost, no-load, tax-efficient ETFs or mutual funds is just fine.

---

[7]Mike Carr's recent book, *Smarter Investing in Any Economy: The Definitive Guide to Relative Strength Investing*, has a great appendix on momentum literature.

Table 4.12 shows a sample Policy Portfolio with ETFs (although some low-cost index funds from Vanguard or Fidelity would work just as well). This is a pretty good portfolio for around 0.3% a year in fees. Hopefully more commodity indexes will come to market and put downward pressure on the fee structure.

Table 4.13 shows a slightly expanded allocation to 10 asset classes that includes small caps, emerging markets, TIPS, and foreign real estate.

And if you want to expand even further to 20 asset classes, you could add micro cap, foreign small cap, foreign bonds, infrastructure, and timber. See Table 4.14.

Table 4.12 Sample Ivy Portfolio Utilizing ETFs

	Harvard and Yale Averaged	Ivy Portfolio	ETF	Expense Ratio
Domestic Stocks	18%	20%	VTI	0.07%
Foreign Stocks	27	20	VEU	0.25
Bonds	14	20	BND	0.11
Real Estate	18	20	VNQ	0.12
Commodities	23	20	DBC	0.83
Total	**100%**	**100%**	—	**0.31%**

Table 4.13 Sample Ivy Portfolio Utilizing ETFs with 10 Asset Classes

	Ivy Portfolio 10	ETFs
Domestic Large Cap	10%	VTI
Domestic Small Cap	10	VB
Foreign Developed Stocks	10	VEU
Foreign Emerging Stocks	10	VWO
Domestic Bonds	10	BND
TIPS	10	TIP
Real Estate	10	VNQ
Foreign Real Estate	10	RWX
Commodities	10	DBC
Commodities	10	GSG
Total	**100%**	—

Table 4.14 Sample Ivy Portfolio Utilizing ETFs with 20 Asset Classes

	Ivy Portfolio	ETFs
Domestic Large Cap	5%	VTI
Domestic Mid Cap	5	VO
Domestic Small Cap	5	VB
Domestic Micro Cap	5	IWC
Foreign Developed Stocks	5	VEU
Foreign Emerging Stocks	5	VWO
Foreign Developed Small Cap	5	GWX
Foreign Emerging Small Cap	5	EWX
Domestic Bonds	5	BND
TIPS	5	TIP
Foreign Bonds	5	BWX
Emerging Bonds	5	ESD
Real Estate	5	VNQ
Foreign Real Estate	5	RWX
Infrastructure	5	IGF
Timber	5	TREE.L
Commodities	5	DBA
Commodities	5	DBE
Commodities	5	DBB
Commodities	5	DBP
Total	**100%**	—

We have attempted to articulate the Ivy Portfolio utilizing ETFs and increasing levels of granularity among the asset classes. We assume that there are some readers who prefer to keep it simple, while others may choose to dig deeper and employ additional asset classes. While the portfolios all have common percentage allocations, an investor may wish to adjust these allocations to fit their individual situation. Those investors with a value bent could switch out some funds for value funds, and by way of example, those individuals that have a lower risk tolerance or are closer to retirement may want a higher allocation of fixed income.

Rebalancing Your Portfolio

We have tackled diversification and then fees and tax efficiency with indexing, but what about discipline and rebalancing? David Swensen, who rebalances to the Policy Portfolio as often as daily, offers his thoughts in *Pioneering Portfolio Management*: "Far too many investors spend enormous amounts of time and energy constructing policy portfolios, only to allow the allocations they established to drift with the whims of the market. . . . Without a disciplined approach to maintaining policy targets, fiduciaries fail to achieve the desired characteristics for the institution's portfolio."

Table 4.15 is a chart of the buy-and-hold Policy Portfolio modeled after the endowment allocations with various rebalance periods. As you can see, the performance and risk numbers are fairly similar. However, there is a clear advantage to rebalancing *sometime* rather than letting the portfolio drift. A simple rebalance can add 0.1 to 0.2 to the Sharpe Ratio.

While a tax-exempt manager like Yale can rebalance monthly (or even daily), it does not make sense for the individual investor. In taxable accounts, time your rebalances with inflows, outflows, and distributions. Buying that new car? Take the money from the asset class that has appreciated the most. Adding some cash? Invest it in the allocation furthest below the target. In a tax-sheltered account make a point to review the portfolio yearly, and then rebalance when it strays.

Table 4.15 Effects of Rebalancing (1985–2008), Fiscal Year Ending June 30th

	Ivy No Rebalance	Ivy Monthly Rebalance	Ivy Yearly Rebalance	Ivy 5-Year Rebalance
Annualized Return	11.03%	11.76%	11.97%	12.05%
Volatility	9.79%	8.51%	8.85%	8.94%
Sharpe (5%)	0.62	0.79	0.79	0.79
Best Year	35.49%	32.00%	34.25%	35.49%
Worst Year	−8.32%	−1.84%	−1.71%	−2.24%
Correlation to H + Y	0.82	0.79	0.80	0.82

Table 4.16   Sample Substitute ETF Portfolios

	ETFs	Substitute ETFs
Domestic Stocks	SPY	VTI
Foreign Stocks	EFA	VEU
Bonds	AGG	BND
Real Estate	IYR	VNQ
Commodities	DBC	RJI

Another potential technique to reduce taxes is tax harvesting. Normally an investor cannot take a loss on a stock/ETF and immediately reinvest the proceeds in the same stock. The IRS has a wash rule that requires a wait time of 30 days. However, it does not say anything about reinvesting in a highly correlated but different index.

If one of the asset classes is facing large losses, the investor can sell the ETF and buy a similar ETF as long as it is based on another index. Switching out two highly correlated ETFs like SPY and VTI is an example. A March 2008 article in *Wealth Manager Magazine* estimated the investor could save 0.5% to 1.5% with this method. (Financial advisors could justify their entire fee by implementing this simple tax strategy.) As always, consult your accountant before executing this strategy. Table 4.16 is an example of easily substitutable ETFs that are based on different indexes.

Many investors could stop with this all-weather Policy Portfolio. In fact, Swensen agrees with this line of thinking, and states an individual investor should shy away from market timing and security selection. That being said, much of Swensen's outperformance was based on alternatives, market timing, and security selection, areas we explore in Parts Two and Three of the book.

Summary

- The Super Endowments on average have returned 4% to 6% more per year than any one asset class.
- An investor can replicate the asset class exposure (without alternatives) of the Super Endowments with liquid indexes.

- An investor can create an all-weather Policy Portfolio with either no-load mutual funds or ETFs.
- The Ivy Portfolio can be constructed with any number of ETFs, and we provide sample portfolios with 5 to 20 asset classes.
- While the exact percentages should be tailored to the individual's situation, the key is an allocation to stocks, bonds, and real assets in line with the endowment percentages.
- A diversified, passive, indexed approach achieves good results, but trails the Super Endowments by about 4% per year for similar volatility.
- Having the discipline to rebalance is important. Tax harvesting could improve the tax efficiency of the portfolio.

Part Two

ALTERNATIVES

Chapter 5

Private Equity

You don't want to be average; it's not worth it, does nothing. In fact, it's less than the market. The question is, 'How do you get to be first quartile?' If you can't, it doesn't matter what the optimizer says about asset allocation.
—Dr. Allan Bufferd, CIO of the MIT endowment
(Foundation and Endowment Investing)

First, the good news. Investing in private equity can offer tremendous returns. Just ask Andreas (Andy) von Bechtolsheim. Andy is a serial entrepreneur (he co-founded Sun Microsystems along with others), but his biggest claim to fame may be an early investment in Google. In 1998, Andy reportedly handed the Google founders Sergey Brin and Larry Page a $200,000 check made out to Google, Inc.—a company that didn't exist yet—and didn't even have a checking account. Ten years later his stake is worth over $2 billion (that's a 150% compound return per year for those counting).

Now, the bad news. Most of the returns in private equity are generated by the top funds (also known as the Golden Circle). This asset class is very difficult for the individual investor to access, and the elite funds are usually only available to institutional investors. It is impossible to access if you are not accredited, currently defined as having a $1 million net worth or an annual income of $200,000 per year or $300,000 if combined with your spouse. The investment vehicle is an illiquid partnership often having a life of 10 or more years, and there is a high bankruptcy rate among portfolio companies. These constraints are no problem for the endowments with huge assets under management and long-term time frames, but they pose major barriers for the individual investor.

Is it even worth the effort? For most individual investors, the answer is a resounding *no*. For investors with more than $50 million in investable assets there are probably better books on how to develop a private equity portfolio. For those willing to gain a better understanding, this chapter looks at the benefits and drawbacks of private equity as an asset class, why it is not a good option for the small investor, and concludes by reviewing publicly listed choices for the individual investor.

What Is Private Equity?

While private equity in the United States has been around since the 1950s, it really began to flourish with the issuance of the prudent man rule by the Department of Labor in 1978 (making it much easier for institutions to invest in private equity). As a result, the past two decades have seen an explosion in private equity from a pool of $100 billion to more than $1 trillion today. This trend has largely been driven by the foundations, endowments, and pension funds attracted to the headline grabbing stories of the fantastic returns available.

There are two main categories of private equity firms—venture capital firms and buyout firms.

Venture capital conjures images of the engineer in his garage building a new technology, or perhaps the new biotechnology company being spun out of a university. Typically the companies seeking venture capital funding are young, not making any money, and could be years away from going public.

Buyouts involve larger companies in more mature industries, and usually the transactions include lots of debt. The companies may be public or private, and the buyer usually takes a controlling stake in the company.

Typically the way a person invests in a fund is as follows. First, an investor (called a limited partner or LP) commits money to a private equity fund run by a general partner (GP). The GP then looks for investment opportunities, and when he finds one he makes a capital call and the LPs send in their money. Even though you committed $1 million, you might be writing checks over the course of a few years for different amounts. When an investment is liquidated (like an initial public offering or IPO), the GP distributes the proceeds to the LPs. Usually the fund has a life of around 10 years, but can be extended to 14.

The timing of the deposits and withdrawals are irregular and unknown at the outset, which makes it incredibly difficult for the individual investor to participate. The investor needs to commit to multiple years (maybe every year in a row for four years) in order to diversify his start date.

Historical Returns and Benchmarking

Benchmarking private equity is a headache in itself. The problem with private equity returns is that annual returns don't mean a thing and can only be known in hindsight when all of the investments have been liquidated or distributed some 10 years later. The returns of a fund are negative in the beginning as money is invested, which is commonly referred to as the J-Curve.

The most commonly accepted way to measure returns is by the internal rate of return (IRR) on a vintage year basis (the year it was formed). This allows the investor to compare all of the private equity funds formed in the same year. This is the best way to measure funds against each other, but only in hindsight years after their formation.

The other way to report performance is time-weighted returns, which is a bit easier to use when looking at private equity on the whole as an asset class. The indexes are published quarterly by pooling *all* the funds in the database regardless of age.

While the methods sound very different, they are fairly close in returns over long periods of time.

There are two main providers of benchmark indexes for private equity: Cambridge Associates and Thomson Venture Economics.

Both have similar returns and are highly correlated, and we use the Cambridge Associates indexes for the purposes of this discussion.

- The Cambridge Associates LLC U.S. Venture Capital Index is based on return data of funds representing over 80% of the total dollars raised by U.S. venture capital managers between 1981 and 2007.
- The Cambridge Associates LLC U.S. Private Equity Index is based on return data of over 600 funds representing more than 70% of the total dollars raised by U.S. leveraged buyout, subordinated debt, and special situation managers between 1986 and 2007.

The indexes are net of annual management fees and the performance fee (also known as carried interest). Typically these fees are around 2% and 20%, respectively. Table 5.1 on pages 88 and 89 shows both indexes along with the Ivy Portfolio, the S&P 500, and the NASDAQ Composite for the calendar year ending December 31st (2008 data is not available yet).

From these numbers alone it looks like the returns are higher than the S&P 500 for both the venture capital and buyout categories, although the venture capital returns are very volatile. Both venture capital and buyout are highly correlated with the NASDAQ Composite. Due to the high correlation with stocks, private equity should be viewed as a component of the larger equity asset class rather than an alternative asset.

But that does not reveal the whole story. Because there is not an investable index, an investor either needs to pick individual funds, or pick a fund of funds (with the additional 1% and 10% fees). When adding the private equity allocations to the Ivy Portfolio we described in the last chapter, venture capital actually decreases the Sharpe Ratio and the buyout increases it only slightly. The increase in return is negated by the increases in volatility and the fact that private equity is largely correlated with stocks.

In a recent study, Ludovic Phalippou and Oliver Gottschalg (2007) examined more than 1,300 private equity funds and found that they outperformed the S&P 500 by about 3% per year. However, once they corrected for survivor bias (including funds that went under or disappeared in the calculation) and fees, the funds underperformed the S&P 500 by about 3% per year.

Another study by Kaplan found that when using the Venture Economics database, buyout fund returns (after fees) are slightly less than those of the S&P 500 and venture capital fund returns are lower than the S&P 500 on an equal-weighted basis, but higher than the S&P 500 on a capital-weighted basis (which means the bigger funds performed better).

Basically, private equity fund returns are about the same as stocks, and the bigger funds perform better. This leads to the question:

If the average fund is not much better than the S&P 500, why does anyone go through all the hassle?

Figures 5.1 and 5.2 show the venture capital and buyout vintage year returns divided up by the top 25%, the median, and the bottom 25% of funds. As you can see, the average fund didn't do much better than the S&P 500. The top 25%, however, did exceptionally better than the average fund, 16% better in venture capital and 8% better in buyout.

Because the rewards of selecting a top quartile fund can be huge. Being able to select the top private equity firms can place you in this rarefied air. In the venture capital category, these top firms include Kleiner Perkins, Sequoia Capital, and New Enterprise Associates. In the buyout category top firms include KKR (Kohlberg Kravis Roberts) Texas Pacific Group, and Blackstone. Relationships

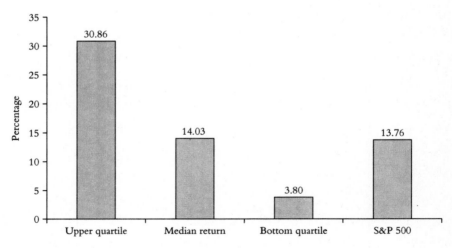

Figure 5.1   VC Vintage Years by Quartile (1986–2003)
SOURCE: Cambridge Associates.

Table 5.1 Benchmark Index Comparison (1986–2007)

	Ivy	S&P 500	NASDAQ Composite	Venture Capital	Buyout	Ivy 85% Venture Capital 15%	Ivy 85% Buyout 15%
1988	18.46%	16.61%	15.41%	3.63%	12.18%	16.24%	17.51%
1989	19.25	31.69	19.26	6.82	10.05	17.40	17.88
1990	−1.10	−3.10	−17.80	1.54	5.21	−0.70	−0.12
1991	18.19	30.46	56.84	20.90	10.08	18.59	16.97
1992	3.88	7.62	15.45	13.28	15.22	5.31	5.51
1993	11.90	10.08	14.75	19.56	24.14	13.05	13.74
1994	1.76	1.32	−3.20	17.79	12.21	4.18	3.33
1995	22.74	37.58	39.92	47.17	24.59	26.48	23.01
1996	19.32	22.96	22.71	40.64	28.66	22.45	20.75
1997	9.96	33.36	21.61	37.66	29.27	14.08	12.84
1998	0.49	28.58	39.63	26.87	15.05	3.60	1.87
1999	14.46	21.04	85.59	275.48	35.36	54.05	17.25
2000	12.73	−9.10	−39.29	29.70	2.01	14.06	11.29
2001	9.74	−11.89	−21.05	−39.00	−11.04	−14.14	−9.94
2002	2.09	−22.10	−31.53	−31.80	−7.56	−2.99	0.63
2003	25.70	28.68	50.01	−2.21	23.37	21.47	25.35
2004	17.44	10.88	8.59	15.40	24.37	17.10	18.56

2005	11.74	4.91	1.37	8.30	28.02	11.23	14.22
2006	12.07	15.80	9.52	17.96	27.06	12.94	14.31
2007	8.06	5.50	9.81	16.25	20.39	9.29	9.92
Annualized Return	10.54%	11.82%	10.97%	17.80%	15.76%	12.47%	11.38%
Volatility	9.15%	16.62%	30.27%	62.31%	12.48%	13.53%	8.98%
Sharpe (5%)	0.66	0.44	0.21	0.21	0.90	0.59	0.77
Correlation to NASDAQ	0.52	0.81	—	0.65	0.65	0.75	0.59
Correlation to Ivy	—	0.65	0.52	0.24	0.57	0.74	0.99

Source: Cambridge Associates.

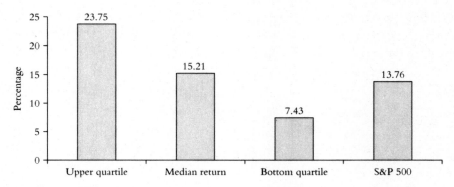

Figure 5.2 Buyout Vintage Years by Quartile (1986–2003)
SOURCE: Cambridge Associates.

mean a lot in this business, and the best firms are shown the best ideas first—a Rolodex matters in venture capital and buyout.

Another recent study by the Boston Consulting Group has shown that the best private equity funds continue to generate the top returns. This is in contrast to mutual funds, where the top performers are often the worst performers in the next period. This is a positive feedback loop. Because the fund outperformed in the beginning, it gets to see the best deals in the next round and invest in better opportunities. The GPs also may add some value here as well, and the better venture capitalists get better deal terms (lower valuations) when negotiating with start-ups (David Hsu, 2002). A start-up would be willing to accept these more stringent terms if the venture capitalists provided superior management, advisory, or reputational inputs.

Table 5.2 shows that results also vary across limited partners (who is investing) and clearly the endowments do better than all others. The median endowment was 23.6%, almost double the entire sample. (If you exclude the top 25% of funds then the average returns for everyone else are quite awful with negative IRRs.)

Basically, unless you are an endowment or can pick the top 20% of private equity funds, you are better off buying a stock index and not dealing with all of the headaches of limited partnerships. Yale has historically returned more than 20% per year in their private equity portfolio. However, these high returns have not been without volatility. Yale's venture portfolio has had years of +700% (2000) and +200% (1980), but years of −40% (2002) as well. (See Table 5.3.) Following a

Table 5.2 Median IRR by LP Type

	Median Return for All Funds in Distribution
Endowments	23.60%
Advisors	20.00
Public Pension Funds	12.30
Other Investors	7.70
Insurance Companies	5.70
Corporate Pension Funds	3.20
Banks and Finance Companies	−0.10
Overall	12.0%

Source: "Smart Institutions, Foolish Choices?: The Limited Partner Performance Puzzle" by Josh Lerner, Antoinette Schoar, and Wan Wang. MIT Sloan Research Paper No. 4523-05, January 2005.

231% return in Yale's buyout portfolio in 1980, it returned −17%, −48%, and −10% the following three years.

Table 5.3 is a good example of the disadvantages of using the Sharpe Ratio as a measure of risk-adjusted performance. Clearly the exceptional performance of the Yale private equity portfolio for the past 20 years is enviable, even with the high volatility. Having the ability to weather the bad years and focus on the long term certainly makes short-term volatility less of a risk factor than it is for most individuals.

However, an additional risk factor mentioned earlier is that as more and more institutions follow Yale into private equity, the returns will naturally decrease as the market becomes more efficient. The market top in 2007 may be one of those times when private equity funds have more money than they know what to do with, which naturally leads to higher buyout prices for target companies, lower deal quality, and lower returns. This boom and bust cycle is common in private equity.

If you *still* want to invest in private equity, the next section looks at the available options.

How to Invest in Publicly Listed Private Equity

We are going to ignore the options available to those people with $50 million who probably have their own family office and have a staff to help select funds. There are certainly a number of private equity

Table 5.3   Yale Private Equity Returns 1988–2006

	Venture Capital	Buyout	International	Total
1988	−0.70%	7.80%	−0.02%	3.30%
1989	−0.30	38.70	13.40	23.40
1990	15.60	7.30	−4.40	11.80
1991	11.60	14.70	−10.00	6.10
1992	28.30	7.20	4.10	14.60
1993	13.60	57.30	−0.20	32.30
1994	20.20	18.70	24.00	24.60
1995	37.80	26.30	13.10	27.00
1996	124.80	31.50	33.70	60.20
1997	37.60	22.10	90.20	36.20
1998	38.00	39.80	1.90	29.00
1999	131.40	8.50	−15.40	37.80
2000	701.00	35.10	38.30	168.50
2001	9.00	−14.70	−3.90	−5.40
2002	−39.90	−11.20	−0.70	−23.30
2003	−13.20	−0.30	1.30	−4.30
2004	−0.70	32.00	21.80	20.60
2005	25.00	32.40	19.00	28.70
2006	16.70	35.90	46.20	32.20
Annualized Return	32.19%	19.05%	12.15%	23.34%
Volatility	160.34%	18.72%	24.86%	39.00%
Sharpe (4.5%)	0.17	0.78	0.31	0.48

Source: "Yale Investment Office: August 2006" by Josh Lerner. Harvard Business School Publishing, January 2007.

fund of funds (FOFs) that could be good options, but we are not in a place to make any recommendations. So what about the little guy?

Private Equity ETFs

There have been some private equity ETFs and a private equity mutual fund that have launched recently. The idea of a U.S.-listed fund is not that interesting because it mainly invests in public companies that are involved in private equity, not the actual funds themselves. A potentially more appealing product became available when PowerShares launched its second private equity ETF to focus on the actual foreign listed private equity *funds*. (If this seems confusing, consider the difference between Fidelity, the management company, and one of Fidelity's actual funds, like Magellan—ticker symbol FMAGX.)

Both ETFs include more than 30 publicly listed companies with direct investments in more than 1,000 private businesses. The indexes are rebalanced and reconstituted quarterly and fund holdings are disclosed every day, giving investors a much higher level of transparency than is often available in traditional private equity funds. Hypothetical index returns are available since 1995, but real-time trading in PowerShares Listed Private Equity (PSP) and PowerShares International Listed Private Equity (PFP) didn't begin until 2006 and 2007, respectively. Unfortunately their launch may have coincided with the top in the private equity market; in 2008 the ETFs are down substantially from their highs.

Some of the benefits of the ETFs are that they are accessible to all investors (no minimums), easily tradable, liquid, marked-to-market every day, and do not have any lockups. The underlying indexes were designed by Red Rocks Capital. The U.S. ETF is based on the Red Rocks Capital Listed Private Equity Index and the foreign ETF is based on the Red Rocks International Listed Private Equity Index.[1]

What do the historical (hypothetical) returns look like?

Table 5.4 indicates that the PSP is highly correlated with the NASDAQ as well as the Cambridge venture capital returns. The PFP is also highly correlated to the NASDAQ, but even more correlated to foreign stocks (MSCI EAFE), which makes sense given that most of the holdings are foreign. In both cases the absolute returns of the portfolio increase along with the volatility resulting in only a minor bump in the Sharpe Ratio. It looks like both ETFs will approximate median venture capital and buyout returns, which are going to behave very similarly to U.S. and foreign equities. While we did not include 2008 data since Cambridge Associates has not reported yet, it was a terrible year for private equity. Both listed ETFs were down over 60%.

---

[1]You can find more information at www.listedprivateequity.com.

Table 5.4 Private Equity ETFs in a Portfolio

	Ivy	S&P 500	EAFE	NASDAQ Composite	Venture Capital	Buyout	PSP	PFP
1996	19.32%	22.96%	6.36%	22.71%	40.64%	28.66%	15.45%	27.91%
1997	9.96	33.36	2.06	21.61	37.66	29.27	48.68	-0.17
1998	0.49	28.58	20.33	39.63	26.87	15.05	16.20	29.70
1999	14.46	21.04	27.3	85.59	275.48	35.36	120.83	82.74
2000	12.73	-9.10	-13.96	-39.29	29.1	2.01	2.70	-1.26
2001	9.74	-11.89	-21.21	-21.05	-39.00	-11.04	-3.09	-14.45
2002	2.09	-22.10	-15.66	-31.53	-31.80	-7.56	-14.09	-9.76
2003	25.70	28.68	39.17	50.01	-2.21	23.37	71.48	67.24
2004	17.44	10.88	20.70	8.59	15.40	24.37	25.76	37.44
2005	11.74	4.91	14.02	1.37	8.30	28.02	6.06	30.40
2006	12.07	15.80	26.86	9.52	17.96	27.06	21.93	29.26
2007	8.06	5.50	11.57	9.81	16.25	20.39	-13.06	3.67
Annualized Return	9.87%	9.32%	8.21%	8.01%	19.29%	16.92%	20.24%	20.39%
Volatility	9.47%	17.78%	18.96%	35.12%	80.33%	15.26%	38.97%	29.95%
Sharpe (5%)	0.62	0.30	0.22	0.11	0.19	0.85	0.42	0.55
Correlation to S&P 500	0.49	—	0.74	0.81	0.38	0.80	0.62	0.61
Correlation to EAFE	0.64	0.74	—	0.79	0.39	0.79	0.62	0.87
Correlation to NASDAQ	0.42	0.81	0.79	—	0.73	0.73	0.85	0.85
Correlation to VC	0.27	0.38	0.39	0.73	—	0.55	0.80	0.67
Correlation to Buyout	0.70	0.80	0.79	0.73	0.55	—	0.60	0.70

Roger Ibbotson takes a look at the Listed Private Equity (LPE) Index and the International LPE Index and their hypothetical history. Ibbotson created his own data series to compare to Red Rocks backfilled series, and found that their results lagged the LPE Indexes by about 5% a year. Whether this is due to this survivor bias, optimization, or simply different construction methodologies is hard to say. Ibbotson recommends, "Institutional investors with access to top quartile managers should continue to use traditional private equity funds to implement a target private equity allocation. For investors who do not have access to top quartile managers and want to include an allocation to private equity, investing in listed private equity is a viable and exciting alternative that, over time, should more accurately reflect the private equity class." (Idzorek, 2007)

Another problem with the foreign listed private equity ETF is tax consequences. Initial research has indicated that there are likely negative ramifications for holding the PFP in a taxable account (see the foreign listed hedge fund section in the next chapter for a full explanation). The recently listed Lehman Opta Private Equity ETN (ticker PPE) could get around the problem due to its structure as a debt vehicle. However, as evidenced by the implosion at Lehman Brothers, you are still exposed to the creditworthiness of the parent company when investing in an ETN. Hopefully, another company will come along and come out with a competing product that avoids all of these issues.

Before you go considering individual foreign listed private equity funds, you need to understand the risk. Many of these funds use leverage and overcommit their capital—beneficial to returns in up markets but devastating in bear markets.[2]

For an interesting examination of one of the oldest business development companies in the United States, Allied Capital, read the book *Fooling Some of the People All of the Time* by hedge fund manager David Einhorn. In the book, Einhorn describes his battle with Allied Capital in which, after his fund shorted the stock, he launched into a vocal public campaign against the company in which he alleged shoddy management and outright fraud.

---

[2]Google Private Equity Holdings ticker symbol PEH, for an example.

We feel like it is simple enough to exclude private equity for the individual investor. For those interested in including private equity in the allocation, it should be viewed as a substitute for part of the domestic and foreign equity allocations.

A tactical approach to private equity could make more sense, which we will take up in Chapter 7. For those looking for more information on private equity we suggest you read the Ibbotson paper, "Private Equity and Strategic Asset Allocation," the Vanguard paper "Understanding Alternative Investments: Private Equity Performance Measurement and Its Role in a Portfolio," and the book *Private Equity as an Asset Class* by Guy Fraser-Sampson.

Summary

- Private equity is a difficult asset class for the individual to access— high investment minimums, closed funds, and lengthy lockups detract from the appeal of private equity.
- Private equity can be lucrative for those able to invest with the top managers.
- Endowments dominate private equity with returns approximately 14% greater than the average investor.
- The average returns of private equity are equity-like with correlations similar to domestic and foreign stocks.
- The difference between top and bottom quartile performers is huge, with most of the returns generated by the top investors.
- The listed ETFs may replicate the median returns of the asset class, but it is too early to tell if they add any value.
- An investor could allocate some of the portfolio to these ETFs with the knowledge that it could simply perform like leveraged U.S. and foreign stocks.

Chapter 6

Hedge Funds

As a client recently said: "There are about 8,000 planes in the air and 100 really good pilots."
—BRIDGEWATER'S RAY DALIO IN *2020 VISION*

lfred Winslow Jones is widely credited with creating the first modern hedge fund in 1949.[1] Jones believed that by shorting some stocks while being long others ("hedging"), and by employing leverage, an investor could outperform conventional mutual funds. He put his thesis to work by raising $100,000 and launching a hedge fund. Unlike their distant mutual fund cousins, the hedge fund structure allows the manager the flexibility and freedom to go long or short any market and spread in the search of the ever elusive alpha.

---

[1]Benjamin Graham had a long-short fund as early as the 1930s that used hedging techniques. Likewise, John Maynard Keynes traded the Chest Fund at King's College in Cambridge, U.K. This long-short macro fund traded stocks, currencies and commodity futures, and while Keynes returned a respectable 9% (excluding dividends and interest) a year from 1927–1945, the fund experienced high volatility of 30% and a number of large and painful drawdowns. However, the U.K. market had negative returns over the time period. The book *Hedgehogging* by Barton Biggs has some good background information.

How about an example? The subprime mortgage meltdown and resulting credit crisis was the big financial story in 2007 and 2008. With the top in U.S. housing prices in place, high default rates on subprime and adjustable rate mortgages resulted in severe liquidity constraints in the banking system. As borrowers became unable to make payments, banks and other financials reported losses in the hundreds of billions. Two of the oldest financial institutions in the United States, Bear Stearns and Lehman Brothers, went under in the wake of the crisis.

Some shrewd investors saw this mess coming. The Paulson Credit Opportunities fund was up 589% in 2007. You read that correctly. Hedge fund manager John Paulson became convinced that investors were far underestimating the risks in the mortgage market as early as 2005. While his positions initially lost money he did more research and only gained conviction in his thesis that serious pain was forthcoming. He launched a fund to focus on betting against risky mortgages, and raised about $150 million from mostly European investors. Funds that he managed were up over $15 billion in 2007, and he stands to make about $3 billion himself (which represents the fattest one-year payday in Wall Street history). This is exactly what hedge funds were designed to do—protect and even profit from the ideas and convictions of the portfolio manager regardless of any single market's direction.

Wouldn't it be nice to have exposure to a fund that protects your portfolio in times like this? Later in this chapter we examine how an individual investor could have invested in the Paulson funds.

First, we are going to take a look at the mysterious world of hedge funds, their returns, and how an investor can possibly gain access to these investment strategies.

A Brief Introduction to Hedge Funds

Up to this point we have been talking about passively investing in asset classes—namely stocks, bonds, real estate, and commodities. Hedge funds are not a separate asset class, but rather investment strategies that trade existing asset classes. The Super Endowments led the push into the alternative space and now allocate about 20% of their portfolios to hedge funds.

Given the potential to deliver positive returns independent of traditional asset classes, hedge fund popularity has exploded. Hedge funds have grown in number from roughly 500 in 1990 to a peak of more than 10,000 in 2007 with industry assets of $2 trillion. See Figure 6.1. In the wake of the 2008 meltdown, the number of hedge funds and assets under management could shrink significantly.

As described in the beginning of this chapter, the first hedge fund is often attributed to Alfred Winslow Jones who built a portfolio of long and short positions in 1949 to lessen the effects of the overall market moves on his portfolio. Historically, hedge funds were formed as limited partnerships or more recently as limited liability companies. Profits and taxes are split according to the interest in the partnership, and flow through to all of the limited partners (the general partner is the manager). Hedge funds can avoid registering under the Securities Act of 1933 or the Securities Exchange Act of 1934 by complying with section 3(c)(1) or 3(c)(7) of the Investment Company Act of 1940. You have to be an accredited investor to gain access to these funds, which means you have to have $1 million in assets or have made $200,000 each of the past two years (or $300,000 if combined with your spouse).

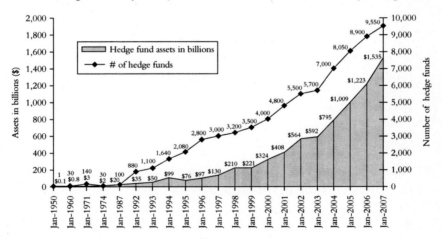

Figure 6.1 Hedge Fund Assets vs. Number of Hedge Funds
SOURCE: Hennessee Group LLC.

Hedge funds can broadly be classified into two categories, directional and nondirectional. Directional will make some bets and have exposure to market direction. Nondirectional neutralizes market risk, and the performance is driven solely by the quality of the manager's picks.

Besides these two broad generalizations, it is difficult to categorize hedge funds. Talking about hedge funds is like describing the average dog. While the average dog may have four legs, a tail, and a preference for table scraps, there is considerable difference between the look and personality of a Beagle, a Great Dane, a Bulldog, and a Greyhound. Because there are so many different types of hedge funds, it is nearly impossible to group them together. And even worse, many funds are mutts and do not conform to a simple style box.

To give you an idea about some of the main categories of hedge funds, Table 6.1 on pages 102 and 103 contains a description of various hedge fund strategies.

Some of the potential benefits of investing in hedge funds include:

- Higher absolute and risk-adjusted returns.
- Low or negative correlation to traditional investments.
- More inefficient markets. (One hedge fund bought up debt from the Republic of the Congo then went after the country in international courts scoring over $30 million in profits.)
- Ability to use leverage, derivatives, and short-selling.
- Fewer constraints on the portfolio.
- Compensation structure—attracts the top talent.

Some of the potential drawbacks of investing in hedge funds are:

- **Liquidity**—many funds have extensive lockups on client assets from one month on out to multiple years.
- **Due diligence**—it takes dozens (if not more than 100) of hours to perform due diligence on individual managers. Multiply 10,000 managers by 100 hours and you've got a major headache.
- **Fees**—the industry standard is 2 and 20, or a 2% annual management fee and a 20% performance fee of the fund's yearly profits. Hedge fund titan Renaissance Technologies charges a 5% management fee and a 44% performance fee. But then again the company has returned more than 35% a year for the past 15 years—*after fees.*

- **Fraud**—while rare, still a risk. The recent Madoff scandal could be as high as $50 billion.
- **Taxes**—most strategies are run without regard to tax implications. Short-term taxation can eat into returns.
- **Transparency**—depends on the manager, but some are very secretive, especially the quantitative shops like D.E. Shaw and Citadel.
- **Herding/Contagion**—risk that funds own the same positions, either because their models result in similar positions or because the managers all go to happy hour together.
- **Attrition**—Roger Ibbotson found that the average life of a hedge fund is two and a half to three years.
- **Leverage**—while some worry about hedge fund fraud and blowups, a simple comparison is illustrative. The two largest hedge fund blowups, Long-Term Capital Management and Amaranth, lost a combined $10 billion. Considering that Enron and Bear Stearns lost well over a combined $100 billion, perhaps this can be viewed as small in comparison.
- **Beta**—some fund managers are simply taking on classic risk premia and charging alpha fees.
- **Closed**—the best managers attract a lot of money then close their doors when assets under management get too large.
- **High water marks**—funds experiencing large drawdowns will often "call it quits" and shut down with huge investor losses.

Fund of Funds

A fund of funds (FOF) raises capital from limited partners and invests the proceeds in several hedge funds. Hedge fund of funds can potentially solve a number of the aforementioned problems. They may offer lower minimums, have more regular liquidity, but most important, they perform the due diligence and manager selection for you. If staffed by a competent group, this function can prove to be worth its weight in gold. Risk is also spread across a number of funds, from a low of a couple of funds to more than 100. However, selecting a FOF group is just like selecting any manager—it all depends on the quality of the manager chosen. Also important, the resulting fund should provide low correlated returns to the investor's current portfolio.

Table 6.1 Description of Strategies

Nondirectional Strategy Descriptions

Equity Market Neutral	Employ individual stock-selection strategies in a market-, industry-, and sector-neutral portfolio to identify return opportunities both long and short. Use quantitative risk control to minimize systematic risk and balance long and short positions.
Convertible Arbitrage	Purchase convertible securities (often bonds) and sell short the underlying common stock to exploit perceived market inefficiency. Neutralize most risk factors outside of the bond's credit risk, earning coupon interest income and short rebates rather than trading on option volatility.
Fixed-Income Arbitrage	Employ strategies to exploit relative mispricings among related fixed-income securities. Strategies typically focus on mispricing relative to a single risk factor—duration, convexity, or yield curve changes—increasing risk control by neutralizing residual factors.

Opportunistic Strategy Descriptions

Long-Short Equity	Take independent long and short stock positions by buying top-tier stocks and shorting those in the bottom tier, seeking to "double alpha." Portfolios often are net long or net short with systematic risk exposure and bets on size, industry, sector, and/or country risk factors.
Emerging Markets	Invest in emerging-market currencies and equity and fixed-income securities with the goal of exploiting perceived market inefficiencies considered to occur more frequently and yielding larger returns. Managers face unique risks in undeveloped markets that are typically characterized by limited information, lack of regulation, and instability.
Dedicated Short Bias	Sell borrowed securities, hoping to later repurchase at a lower price and return them to the lender. Short selling earns a profit if prices fall. Interest is also received on the cash proceeds from the short sale.

Global Macro

Bet on global macroeconomic events, anticipating shifts in government policy or market trends. Focus primarily on directional trades using currencies, derivatives, stocks, and bonds, rapidly shifting between perceived opportunities while taking on significant market risk (more when leveraged).
Success depends directly on the skill of the manager.

Managed Futures

Rely on technical or fundamental trend-following models to invest in global options and futures based on currencies, interest rate and index derivatives, and commodities. Risks include unanticipated commodity shocks, incorrect forecasts, and poor trade timing or positioning.

Event Driven

Profit on firm events such as acquisitions, mergers, tender and/or exchange offers, capital structure change, the sale of entire assets or business lines, and entry into or exit from new markets. Returns tend to be highly dependent on a manager's ability to spot these opportunities. Do not hedge against factors such as a weak merger environment or the risk that deals are not completed.

Source: "Understanding alternative investments: A primer on hedge fund evaluation" by The Vanguard Group, 2006.

Academic Fund Managers

Swensen is not alone—some of the best funds are run by academics. The fourth biggest (and very likely the best) hedge fund is run by the mathematician James Simons. Founded in the 1980s, the Long Island-based fund Renaissance Technologies now manages over $30 billion. The flagship Medallion fund has consistently returned 35% a year after a 5% management fee and a 44% incentive fee (and has been closed to new investors since 1993)! With the exception of 1989, the fund has never had a down year. Simons is famous for only hiring Ph.D.s, and the fund's employees are largely former scientists from around the world with backgrounds in mathematics, physics, astrophysics, and statistics. Purely quant driven, Simons states, "We decided that systematic trading was best. Fundamental trading gave me ulcers." Simons shook the investment world recently by announcing a new fund with a total capacity of $100 billion.

The sixth biggest hedge fund D.E. Shaw was founded by Columbia University computer science professor David Shaw in 1988. Also quantitatively focused, the fund returned most investor capital in 1997.

Another famous academic is Richard Thaler, a professor of behavioral economics at University of Chicago's Graduate School of Business. He cofounded Fuller & Thaler Asset Management in 1993, and the company now manages more than $3 billion. Thaler is the author of numerous texts in the field of behavioral finance, and also the author of the recently published *Nudge: Improving Decisions about Health, Wealth, and Happiness*.

Ed Thorp, who obtained his Ph.D. from UCLA and is one of the developers of card counting theory in blackjack (he wrote the book *Beat the Dealer*), ran a successful hedge fund for many years. The fund, Princeton Newport Partners, returned 15% a year for 20 years with no down years and volatility around 10%. Thorp's fund only recorded three down

Academic Fund Managers (*Continued*)

months in those 20 years and was the first market neutral and quantitative hedge fund. The Harvard endowment was an early investor. (As an interesting aside, the most famous bond manager in the world—PIMCO's Bill Gross—paid his way through college counting cards in Lake Tahoe.)

Of course, there is also the flip side to this story including famous blowups like the one at Long-Term Capital Management (LTCM) in 1998; *When Genius Failed* by Roger Lowenstein is a great book on the topic. The roster of LTCM founders included two Nobel Laureates as well as a number of star traders from Salomon Brothers. The fund was the first fund to raise $1 billion and had great returns from 1994–1997, but had catastrophic losses of more than 95% in 1998 due to massive amounts of leverage and positions moving in unison in the wrong direction. The Harvard endowment was an investor in LTCM as well.

The biggest drawback of a FOF is fees. By the time an individual receives his returns from a FOF, the underlying hedge funds have collected 2% and 20%, and the FOF layers on another 1% and 10%. Let's do the math with the Ivy Portfolio. Since 1990, it has returned about 10% a year. To achieve similar returns at a FOF level, the underlying hedge funds must return:

$$\text{Ivy Portfolio} = 10\%$$

$$\text{Gross returns of FOF} = (10\% + 1\%)/(100\% - 10\%) = 12.22\%$$

$$\text{Gross returns of hedge funds} = (12.22\% + 2\%)/(100\% - 20\%) = 17.75\%$$

So, the underlying hedge funds would have to return an additional 7% a year to achieve the same return as the basic buy and hold Ivy Portfolio. To achieve these returns, the FOF manager must either select a lot of *really* skilled alpha producers, leverage up the portfolio, or do a combination of both. These massive fees work against the individual investor.

A note about fees—they are relative to what is delivered. Some mutual funds and ETFs are expensive at 0.75% a year. Renaissance Technologies is probably cheap at a 5% management fee and a 44% performance fee. It all depends on the edge a manager has and the alpha he produces. Warren Buffett famously set up his partnership with a 25% performance fee over a 6% hurdle. That way he only got paid if his clients made more than 6% a year. A good rule of thumb is that the alpha should be split 25% to 33% to the manager, and 75% to 66% to the investor, regardless of how it is structured.

Now that we have talked about the pros and cons of hedge funds, the real question is: How have hedge funds performed over the years? For every Tudor, Caxton, and Renaissance Technologies, there are also plenty of Amaranths and Long-Term Capital Managements. Let's look at the data.

Problems with Using Hedge Fund Databases to Track Performance

One of the problems with defining hedge fund performance is that there is no index like there is for other asset classes. Because a hedge fund is a private partnership, there is no requirement to report or disclose performance numbers. There are numerous firms that compile their versions of hedge fund indexes, each with different rules. They have different numbers of underlying funds (60–5,000), some collect the data themselves while some do not, some include managed futures and some do not. No one really knows how many funds are in existence.

A database is simply a collection of hedge funds and their returns, and very likely will be replete with survivorship and backfilling biases. In a recent study, PerTrac estimates the number of funds from 11 databases at 22,000 (Benjamin, 2008). The estimating is complicated by the fact that a single manager can manage several hedge funds. Very few funds report to more than two or three databases, and only one reported to all of them. Over half of the funds only reported to one database.

Some of the biases included in the databases are:

- **Selection**—Manager can choose if and to what database he reports performance.
- **Survivor**—Hedge fund managers no longer in existence may be excluded from the database. This can include funds that blew up as well as funds that stopped reporting due to good performance.
- **Backfill**—Database provider backfills performance history of hedge fund introduced into index.
- **Liquidation**—Funds that go out of business stop reporting performance in advance of shutting their doors. They are still in the database but their last few months of bad performance are omitted.

Most studies have found that these biases add up to more than 4% in overstated returns. Add that to the fact that most databases only have data for 10–15 years, and you can see how these databases have lots of problems (Fung and Hsieh (2006), Malkiel and Saha (2005), Ibbotson and Chen (2005), and Van and Song (2004)).

Using Hedge Fund Indexes to Track Returns

In contrast to hedge fund databases, hedge fund *indices* calculate index returns on a going-forward basis, and any additions and deletions are reported in real time. Investable indices, if constructed properly, should be free from these aforementioned biases.

When hedge funds are combined into a portfolio, many of the unique and desirable hedge fund features diversify away. Indices no longer resemble hedge funds, but are mainly composed of stock and bond risk. You do not want to pay high fees for beta exposure. Some of the numerous hedge fund indices are listed in Table 6.2.

An example of the differences in indexing can be seen in Table 6.3. For example, the February 2000 results for the long/short EACM and Zurich indices painted a very different picture for the universe of long/short funds. If you were following the Zurich index, it looked like long/short had a great month at 20.48%. The EACM Index conveys different information, with a reported return of −1.56%, a difference of over 20%!

Table 6.2 Description of Indexes

Index Provider	Launch Date of Indices	Start Date of Indices Database	Number of Funds in the Database	Number of Funds in the Indices	Rebalancing Frequency
Altvest	2000	1993	+3,200	+2,200	Monthly
Barclay Group	2003	1997	+4,460	4,400	Monthly
CISDM	1994	1990	+7,600	3,892	Monthly
CSFB/Tremont	1999	1994	+4,500	413	Quarterly
EACM	1996	1996	100	100	Annual
EDHEC	2003	1997	NA	NA	Quarterly
Hennessee	1987	1987	+3,000	900	Annual
HF Net	1998	1976–1995*	+5,000	+3,600	Monthly
HFR	1994	1990	2,300	+1,600	Monthly
MSCI	2002	2002	+2,000	+2,000	Quarterly
Van Hedge	1994	1988	+6,700	+2,000	Monthly

Source: EDHEC Risk and Asset Management Research Centre (http://www.edhec-risk.com).
*Depends on strategy.

Hedge Fund Research, Inc. (HFRI) publishes indices that track the hedge fund universe back to 1990, and we will examine the relative performance here because it represents one of the longest histories for a hedge fund index. The HFRI Weighted Composite Index (HFRIFWI) is an equal-weighted index of more than 1,600 hedge funds, excluding fund of funds, and results in a very general picture of performance across the hedge fund industry. The HFRI Fund of Fund Composite Index (HFRIFOF) is a similar index with approximately 750 fund of funds included.

A couple of characteristics of the index methodology must be noted. Because the indices are equal-weighted and there is no required asset-size minimum for fund inclusion, the results will be biased to smaller fund returns. There will be some survivorship bias in the results due to poorly performing managers electing not to report their returns once the results turn negative. It is difficult to determine the effects of this bias, but a comparison of the HFRX indices (the investable version,

Table 6.3 Variance in Index Returns

Investment Styles	Maximum Differences	Date	Indices and Corresponding Returns	Versus
Convertible Arb	7.55%	Dec. 01	EACM (−6.93%)	Hennessee (0.62%)
CTA	5.09	Feb. 99	CSFB (−0.54)	HF Net (4.55)
Distressed	6.99	Feb. 00	EACM (1.23)	Zurich (8.22)
Emerging Markets	19.46	Aug. 98	MAR (−26.65)	Altvest (−7.20)
Equity Market Neutral	5.00	Dec. 99	Hennessee (0.20)	Van Hedge (5.20)
Event Driven	5.06	Aug. 98	CSFB (−11.77)	Altvest (−6.71)
Fixed Income Arb	10.48	Oct. 98	HF Net (−10.28)	Van Hedge (0.20)
FOFs	8.01	Dec. 99	MAR (2.41)	Altvest (10.42)
Global Macro	14.17	Oct. 98	CSFB (−11.55)	Altvest (2.62)
Long/Short Equity	22.04	Feb. 00	EACM (−1.56)	Zurich (20.48)
Merger Arb	2.71	Sept. 01	EACM (−4.32)	HF Net (−1.61)
Relative Value	10.47	Sept. 98	EACM (−6.08)	Van Hedge (4.40)
Short Selling	21.13	Feb. 00	Van Hedge (−24.30)	EACM (−3.17)

Source: EDHEC Risk and Asset Management Research Centre (www.edhec-risk.com).

available only since 2003) and the HFRI (a financially engineered time series) indices could give a clear view of any tracking error. An analysis we conducted found the effect to be over 4% for each substrategy—a very material difference.

A further examination by Greenwich Alternative Investments found similar results in most of the investable indices (Johnson, 2007). The investable indices will not have the best hedge funds in them because these top performers are sufficiently capitalized and have closed the doors to new investors. One of the problems with the investable indices is that they are constructed with liquidity and investability in mind rather than representativeness of the industry.

Evaluating Historical Returns

Remember, these results must be taken with a grain of salt. With the understanding that the hedge fund indices returns will likely be overstated versus the investable versions, we present the year-by-year results of the HFRI and FOF indices in Table 6.4. (There will also be a slight diversification benefit from the index. It is like a FOF without the fees.)

The results of the HFRIFOF and the HFRIFWI are impressive as standalone products. However, adding the HFRIFOF index to the Ivy Portfolio does little to improve risk-adjusted returns. The reason is that the risk factors are very similar to a balanced portfolio. The HFRIFWI does a slightly better job, but once you factor in the underperformance of the investable version it maintains little appeal. Overall, we believe that these indices are fairly good proxies for the hedge fund universe, but the investable indices are not good investment choices.

Comparing Credit Suisse/Tremont

The Credit Suisse/Tremont Hedge Fund Index is asset-weighted, and all funds must have a minimum of $50 million in assets under management, a minimum one-year track record, and current audited financial statements. There are approximately 5,000 funds in the database, 500 funds in the index, no FOFs are included, and performance is net of

Table 6.4 HFR Returns for the Calendar Year Ending December 31, 2008

	S&P 500	Ivy	HFRIFOF	HFRIFWI	Ivy 80% FOF 20%	Ivy 80% Hedge 20%
1990	−3.10%	−1.10%	17.53%	5.81%	2.62%	0.28%
1991	30.46	18.19	14.50	32.19	17.45	20.99
1992	7.62	3.88	12.33	21.22	5.57	7.35
1993	10.08	11.90	26.32	30.88	14.79	15.70
1994	1.32	1.76	−3.48	4.10	0.72	2.23
1995	37.58	22.74	11.10	21.50	20.41	22.49
1996	22.96	19.32	14.39	21.10	18.33	19.68
1997	33.36	9.96	16.20	16.79	11.21	11.33
1998	28.58	0.49	−5.11	2.62	−1.41	0.13
1999	21.04	14.46	26.47	31.29	16.63	17.59
2000	−9.10	12.73	4.07	4.98	10.99	11.18
2001	−11.89	9.74	2.80	4.62	−7.23	−6.87
2002	−22.10	2.09	1.02	−1.45	1.78	1.38
2003	28.68	25.70	11.61	19.55	22.88	24.47
2004	10.88	17.44	6.86	9.03	15.33	15.76
2005	4.91	11.74	7.49	9.30	10.89	11.25

(Continued)

Table 6.4 HFR Returns for the Calendar Year Ending December 31, 2008 (*Continued*)

	S&P 500	Ivy	HFRIFOF	HFRIFWI	Ivy 80% FOF 20%	Ivy 80% Hedge 20%
2006	15.80	12.07	10.39	12.89	11.73	12.23
2007	5.50	8.06	10.25	9.96	8.5	8.45
2008	−36.77	−29.76	−18.30	−19.97	−27.47	−27.80
Return	7.34%	7.11%	8.24%	11.71%	7.40%	8.08%
Volatility	19.85%	12.80%	10.66%	12.88%	11.77%	12.33%
Sharpe 4%	0.17	0.24	0.40	0.60	0.29	0.33
Max Drawdown	−44.73%	−35.67%	−20.82%	−19.86%	−32.41%	−32.42%
Correl to S&P	1.00	0.76	0.56	0.75	0.77	0.79
Correl to Ivy	0.76	1.00	0.67	0.77	0.99	0.99

Source: Hedge Fund Research, Inc., © 2008, www.hedgefundresearch.com.

Table 6.5   CS/Tremont Return Statistics (January 1994–December 2008)

Inception-to-date Statistics	Annualized Total Return	Annualized Volatility	Sharpe Ratio
CS/Tremont Hedge Fund Index	8.79%	7.98%	0.62
Convertible Arb	5.55	6.85	0.25
Dedicated Short Bias	−0.67	17.00	−0.27
Emerging Markets	6.72	15.90	0.18
Equity Market Neutral	5.57	11.06	0.16
Event Driven	9.75	6.10	0.97
Distressed	10.84	6.72	1.04
Multi-Strategy	9.22	6.51	0.83
Risk Arbitrage	6.97	4.31	0.73
Fixed Income Arb	3.54	6.01	−0.05
Global Macro	12.46	10.60	0.81
Long/Short Equity	9.70	10.25	0.57
Managed Futures	7.08	11.93	0.27
Multi-Strategy	7.27	5.45	0.63

Source: Copyright 2008, Credit Suisse/Tremont Index LLC.

all fees. Table 6.5 details the performance of the index along with all of the subindexes. A quick glance shows how difficult shorting is with negative annual returns. Multistrategy, global macro, event driven, and market neutral have the best risk-adjusted returns.

It is interesting to note that while the return and risk numbers for the HFR Index are a little different from those of the CS/Tremont, the Sharpe Ratio is nearly identical at around 0.6.

While the composition of the index has changed a little bit over the years, the largest component has remained long/short equity. (See Table 6.6.)

Options to Invest in Hedge Funds

So you have decided that you want to invest in hedge funds. What now?

The first option is to do a ton of research and pick some of the private funds out of the universe of over 10,000. This choice makes sense

Table 6.6 Description Sector Allocation

Strategy	Allocation
Convertible Arbitrage	2%
Dedicated Short Bias	1
Emerging Markets	8
Equity Market Neutral	5
Event Driven	25
Fixed-Income Arbitrage	5
Global Macro	11
Long/Short Equity	28
Managed Futures	4
Multi Strategy	11

Source: Copyright 2008, Credit Suisse/Tremont Index LLC.

if you are an investment professional, or an individual investor who has a lot of time to do the research and in need of a hobby. Otherwise, it is probably not the best course of action.

Investing in a private FOF is the next choice, but again, unless you are a professional or have hired one you trust, the problem of selecting a good manager still exists.

With both of these choices you still have to be accredited, be able to invest the minimum amount, and deal with liquidity and lockup issues.

The next choice, becoming more available by the day, is to invest in the publicly available alternative funds in the United States. Funds in the United States are starting to look more and more hedge-like.

The last choice is one that is not talked about much here in the United States, and that is investing in foreign listed hedge funds. (Listed just means that the fund is traded on an exchange.) Never heard of them? Don't be surprised, neither has almost anyone else in the United States.

Next we examine the growing U.S. listed alternatives space, followed by the developed foreign listed hedge fund space.

U.S. Funds

U.S. listed funds are currently much less interesting than the foreign funds we discuss in the next section. The funds listed in the United States aren't real hedge funds, but take one of three forms: mutual fund, closed-end fund, or ETF. Mutual funds are open ended, meaning they allow investors to deposit and withdraw their funds every day and their assets under management vary with these levels. Closed-end funds list on an exchange with a fixed amount of assets that trade just like stocks. Because of this property, the trading price each day typically deviates to some extent from their net asset value (NAV). Below we will detail a few of the names that are now available and an example in each category. The overviews are split into two sections—funds with little correlation to the Ivy Portfolio and funds that are replacements for part of the portfolio (like stocks).

You have to be careful with these funds, and often the sponsor believes the search for alpha equals the right to charge higher fees. First we will take a look at listed funds that could be added to an already diversified portfolio (low correlation), then the funds that could serve as substitutes for part of the portfolio (replacement funds).[2]

Currencies Most portfolio managers would agree that currency markets do not contain any beta by nature since they are a zero-sum game. Deutsche Bank (DB) takes a different position, and it set out to create a currency benchmark based on three widely accepted strategies: carry, value, and momentum.[3]

- Carry: buys high interest rate currencies and shorts low interest rate currencies.
- Momentum: buys currencies going up and shorts currencies going down.

---

[2]As an interesting aside, the mutual fund with the longest running streak of no down years in 18 years is the T Rowe Price Capital Appreciation Fund (PRWCX). Next in line are the Gabelli ABC (GABCX) and First Eagle Overseas (SGOVX) funds at 14 years. All three lost money in 2008.

[3]A good review is the paper "Do Professional Currency Managers Beat the Benchmark?" that will be linked to on the book web site.

- Value: buys currencies under fair value as determined by purchasing power parity, and shorts those above the value.

Returns for the three indexes are fairly similar, and the DB Currency Returns Index is an equal-weighted index of the three strategies. The only product to come to market so far is the DB Carry ETF (DBV). These are great offerings, but it would be nice to be able to invest in the total index rather than just the carry index. Hopefully DB will bring more of these to market as they exhibit equity-like returns with bond-like volatility and drawdown and little or negative correlation to existing asset classes. There have been some tax issues with DBV, and there have been some competing carry ETFs to hit the market recently that may be more tax friendly.

Hedged Equity More and more long/short mutual funds are coming to market, which is a good sign (Vanguard even has a market neutral fund). The TFS Market Neutral Fund (TFSMX, www.tfscapital.com) launched in 2004, and it has returned about 8% annualized since inception with a low volatility of around 9%. Most important, when taking a look at most of the down moves in the S&P, the fund has held up nicely (with the exception of the quant mess in the summer of 2007). Currently the fund has over $165 million in 513 longs and $112 million in 355 shorts.

The Hussman Strategic Growth Fund (HSGFX, www.hussmanfunds. com) has annualized returns of around 8% since the launch in 2000, but most important, it was up in 2000, 2001, and 2002. For a diversifying hedge fund this is good to see, as you don't want to just layer on more equity exposure. Even though the fund has had returns in the single digits for the past few years, Hussman has not had a down year since inception, and the volatility is bond-like.

Managed Futures This category could be included in either the low correlation category or the replacement category depending on the investor's current allocation. Managed futures are a great addition to a portfolio that doesn't already have commodities, but in the Ivy Portfolio it should be a replacement for part of the commodity allocation.

Managed futures are an example of alternative beta, and roughly 70% of managed futures programs are simple rules-based trend followers that are highly correlated to one another. Alternative beta is an untraditional risk exposure that is simple and rules based. Typically, alternative beta is a strategy or factor that was once considered an alpha source but has since been commoditized.

The approach is nothing more than a tactical approach to one asset class (commodities, although some programs add in some financials), and you can read more on this topic in the next chapter. We expect to see a number of managed futures offerings hit the market in the next year or two, which should work to put pressure on the fees charged. While most passive indexes will drift down to about 0.1% to 0.3% in fees, the alternative beta funds like this will drift down to 0.5% to 0.75%. For some good background reading, check out the research pieces on the Bridgewater site (www.bwater.com), especially "Hedge Funds Levering Betas." Bridgewater found a number of hedge fund strategies could be explained simply with some common risk factors, including convertible arbitrage, emerging markets, merger arbitrage, distressed, and fixed-income arbitrage.

Rydex (www.rydex.com) launched the first managed futures offering in a mutual fund structure in the United States (RYMFX). There have been other public managed futures offerings, but for the most part they are difficult to invest in for the ordinary investor and often very expensive. Frontier was a pioneer, and it had to go through the ringer to make its funds available to the public. Rydex's prospectus is over 500 pages long.

The logic of the Rydex fund is based on a simple moving average model developed by Victor Sperandeo and named the S&P Diversified Trend Indicator (DTI). The fund takes a long/short approach to the commodities and financials. For a more in-depth examination of the subject the reader can check out Sperandeo's book *Trader Vic on Commodities*, as well as the next chapter.

Very recently an ETN (ticker: LSC) came out with a lower fee structure on the sister index to the DTI, the CTI (it excludes interest rates and financials).

Stock Replacement Funds—Go Anywhere There are some alpha generators in the mutual fund space, but mostly these funds should be considered replacement funds. Because they will largely be composed of stock risk, it is best to substitute some of the equity allocation with some of these funds if you want, otherwise you could be layering on additional risk. Similar to the "go anywhere" funds Swensen mentioned in the Yale chapter, these funds will likely perform in a manner independent of the indices.

The Fairholme Fund (FAIRX, http://www.fairholmefunds.com) has been performing lights out since the 2000 launch with annualized returns of over 10%. The manager, Bruce Berkowitz, runs a concentrated portfolio that doesn't hug the benchmarks, and his top five positions account for roughly 50% of the fund. Even more important, he has 100% of his investment wealth in the fund.

A similar manager is Ken Heebner, who runs the CGM Focus Fund (CGMFX, http://cgmfunds.com). Like Berkowitz, he runs a concentrated portfolio with the top 10 holdings accounting for over 80% of the fund's assets. Heebner can short as well and has been compounding the fund at about 15% for the past 10 years. There will be some volatility here, and declines like the 18% drop in 2000 can be expected. Then again, you would have had that 80% year in 2007. Often, managers start to trail off when assets get too large, and it will be interesting to see if Heebner keeps the fund open as assets pass $8 billion. Recently, Heebner announced his intentions to launch a hedge fund with targeted assets of $5 billion.

Merger Arbitrage While Yale allocates to merger arbitrage strategies, we feel that the appeal of this strategy is limited. If you're interested, there are a few funds that exist in this space—MERFX, GABCX, and ARBFX. This seems like another example of alternative beta, and if an ETF ever came out with a low fee structure, that would be a better option. All of the value comes with predicting which mergers will go through, a difficult task with a great amount of competition.

Covered Calls The covered call space is similar to the merger arbitrage space. There are a few mutual funds here (GATEX, FUND), but a solid approach would be to screen for the many closed-end funds that use this strategy and often trade at discounts to their NAV. As always, be careful and read the prospectus as some of these funds can be quite leveraged.

Rotation Strategies We take this subject up at length in the next chapter. There are a number of funds launching that focus on momentum and rotation strategies. They have various levels of appeal due to differences in strategy, fees, implementation, and asset classes utilized. In general, we are proponents of this category of funds, but discretion is required in selecting the right ones. A few examples are:

International
- Rydex International Rotation Fund (RYFHX).
- Claymore/Zack's Country Rotation (CRO).

Sector
- DWA Technical Leaders (PDP).
- DWA Balanced (DWAFX).
- VL Industry Rotation (PYH).
- VL Timeliness (PIV).
- Rydex Sector Rotation Fund (RYSRX).
- Claymore/Zack's Sector Rotation (XRO).

Dividend Funds (or a Former Alpha Generator) Hundreds of newsletters, books, and investment strategies focus on dividends, and why not? They certainly tell a good story—if a company has the ability to return cash to investors it is clearly doing something right. Many investors see dividends as a safe haven when in reality they are not.

The "Dogs of the Dow" is a good example. This strategy simply selects the 10 highest yielding stocks out of 30 from the Dow Jones Industrial Average Index (DJIA). Michael O'Higgins generally gets most of the recognition for popularizing the strategy in a book published in 1991 titled *Beating the Dow*.[4] This strategy outperformed the benchmark DJIA handily until the time of the publication, and subsequent performance of the strategy since 1991 has been in-line with the DJIA Index (as of June 2008 this is one of the worst years on record for

---

[4]O'Higgins was not the first to come up with the strategy; John Slatter mentions it is his 1991 book *Safe Investing: How to Make Money without Losing Your Shirt* and an article by H.G. Schneider published in the June 1951 *Journal of Finance* documents a strategy of investing in low P/E Dow stocks.

the strategy). Many observers believed that this was a case of too much money flooding into a strategy and rendering it ineffective.[5] However, a structural change in the markets is more likely the reason dividends have lost their predictive ability.

Dividends are only one way of returning capital to shareholders. Share repurchases are another such method (see Microsoft), and since they are not taxed like dividends, it can be argued they are a more efficient way of returning profits. Buybacks represent about half of all shareholder payouts and have increased steadily since the early 1980s. There is a structural reason for this, and it is due primarily to the SEC instituting rule 10b–18 in 1982—providing a safe harbor for firms conducting repurchases from stock manipulation charges. See Grullon and Michaely (2002) for more information on the impact of Rule 10b–18.

A paper by Boudoukh, Michaely, Richardson, and Roberts titled, "On the Importance of Payout Yield" examined the payout yield and net payout yield, whose formula is:

Payout Yield = $ spent on dividends + $ spent on share repurchases

Net Payout Yield = $ spent on dividends + $ spent on share repurchases − $ raised through new share issues

The authors find that "the widely documented decline in the predictive power of dividends for excess stock returns is due largely to the omission of alternative channels by which firms distribute and receive cash from shareholders." Additionally, while dividend yield has lost its predictive ability over time, the payout yield has remained a robust indicator for excess stock return.[6]

This is an example of how an investor needs to continually be aware of structural changes in the market and not be sold on investment stories that simply sound reasonable.

Now, on to the more interesting funds!

---

[5]At one time Merrill had a unit trust named the Select-10 with over $10 billion AUM.

[6]An even more comprehensive paper is scheduled for publication in the *Journal of Finance* in late 2008: "Asset Growth and the Cross-Section of Stock Returns" by Schill, Gulen, and Cooper.

Foreign Listed Hedge Funds[7]

Remember the Paulson example mentioned earlier in which one of his funds returned over 500% in 2007? No way you could invest in that fund, right? Huge minimum investment size and accreditation rules eliminate most of us. However, if you have a brokerage account, it is as easy as buying a stock. Thames River (up 25% in 2007) and Dexion Alpha (up 12%) are two examples of funds an individual investor can buy that held the Paulson funds. In fact, about 20% of the foreign listed funds had an allocation to at least one Paulson fund in 2007.

Instead of private partnerships, the foreign listed hedge fund sector is similar to the closed-end fund space in the United States. There are more than 50 funds with assets over $20 billion, and growth of assets under management is substantial—in 2007 the listed fund sector grew by 50%. While most funds are listed in London as FOFs, individual funds should see more listings in the future as the public becomes comfortable with the space. Six hedge funds and FOFs are currently included in the FTSE indexes. There are also funds listed in Amsterdam, Switzerland, and Canada.

To date, there are no listed hedge funds in the United States. Rumors last year were that William Ackman is considering launching a fund. He runs the $6 billion Pershing Square Capital Management and has stated, "I'm a believer that certain hedge funds should be publicly traded." The British company Man Group was lined up to become the first firm to list a hedge fund on the NYSE last fall, but delayed the offering as two of the underlying managers, Tykhe Capital and AHL Core had poor performance.

Why would a company want to pursue a listing? It gives the investment manager a permanent source of capital, allows the manager to conduct strategies without worrying about short-term deposits and withdrawals, and allows the manager to market to a new demographic.

---

[7]There appear to be potential tax issues that U.S. investors who invest in these funds must analyze and resolve. We present the information in this chapter for two reasons. First, we include the information as an educational introduction to the sector and an essay on how far the United States is behind the rest of the world in listing these funds. Two, we hope that a product comes to market for U.S. investors that will alleviate some of the concerns listed in the following pages.

The first listings were Alternative Investment Strategies and Altin AG in 1996 which each raised about $50 million. The modern sector really dates from the launch of Dexion Absolute in December 2002. Despite raising just £34 million (US$63 million) at launch, following two secondary issues in the next 18 months, assets increased seven-fold to £240 million ($445 million), with much of the new money from new investors. A strong performance record has fueled further growth, both organically and through further secondary issues, and assets now stand at £870 million ($1.6 billion) with a further fund-raising under consideration. The success of Dexion Absolute and its underlying manager, Harris Alternatives (based in Chicago), has been a powerful advertisement for the U.K. listed fund of hedge funds product.

Due to the exchange traded nature of these funds, they also trade at premiums or discounts to their NAV. A smart approach to these funds is to buy them when they trade at discounts (Boussard hit a 30% discount in 2008), and sell them when they trade at premiums. If you recall, Harvard and Yale employ similar approaches in their portfolios with closed-end funds in the United States. Most funds that launch today have provisions for share buyback programs to manage the discounts to NAV.

Another benefit of these funds is that there are no accreditation requirements for the individual investor. Many funds that are impossible for the individual to invest in due to high minimums or a fund's closure to new investors can be accessed through the listed FOFs. Table 6.7 shows the top 15 funds by assets under management (AUM).

This section details some of the largest funds and funds of funds listed on the exchanges. The investor can find more information on the fund web sites including fact sheets, interviews, and returns. If you are located in the United States, you may have to forget momentarily where you are located to access the web sites. Likewise, some of the European banks cover the space (ABN AMRO, Dresdner Kleinworst).

Why hasn't a hedge fund listed in the United States? There are a number of potential reasons, but a few stand out. One manager said it was because the mutual fund lobby is too powerful. Another manager mentioned the listing requirements are much less onerous abroad.

Table 6.7 Largest Funds and FOFs

Company	Type	Exchange	AUM (£m)
Dexion Absolute	FOF	LSE	1,492
MW TOPS	HF	AEX	960
BH Macro	HF	LSE	876
Boussard & Gavaudan	HF	AEX	746
BH Global	HF	LSE	507
Absolute Invest	FOF	SWX	459
Thames River	FOF	LSE	393
Ashmore Global	HF	LSE	376
Castle Alternative	FOF	SWX	324
Alternative Investment Strategies	FOF	LSE	323
Goldman Sachs Dynamic Opportunities	FOF	LSE	316
Third Point Offshore	HF	LSE	272
Absolute Return	FOF	LSE	263
CMA Global Hedge	FOF	LSE	242
Acencia Debt	FOF	LSE	233

Source: AMN AMRO Bank.
FOF = Fund of Funds
HF = Hedge Fund
LSE = London Stock Exchange
SWX = Swiss Exchange
AEX = Euronext Amsterdam Exchange

Whatever the reason, it will be a great day when the first brave manager lists a hedge fund in the United States.

Individual Hedge Funds

This section details two of the larger individual funds. While the individual funds have historically trailed the fund of funds in number of funds listed and assets under management, recently there have been more individual launches and assets are approaching parity with the FOFs.

Fund: Third Point Offshore Ltd
  Manager: Third Point LLC
  Web site: www.thirdpointpublic.com
  Location: New York City
  Listing: London Stock Exchange (LSE)
  Symbol: TPOG (Yahoo TPOG.L)
  Fund AUM ($): approximately $150 million
  Currency share classes: £, $, €

The Third Point Offshore fund is a global long/short equity fund launched in July 2007 with $500 million in assets that trades on the London Stock Exchange. It invests all of its assets in the Third Point Offshore Fund (the Master Fund), which was founded in 1995 by Daniel Loeb and is an event-driven bottom-up fundamental value investor. Loeb runs a long/short strategy, featuring distressed and merger arbitrage situations in the United States and some European mid- and large-cap equities. Third Point targets net long exposure of 20% to 80% and 80–100 long positions and 50–60 short positions.

Since the launch in 1995, the fund has returned about 20% a year, more than 10% a year above the S&P 500. Even more amazing is that Loeb has achieved this with less volatility than the S&P 500. Third Point is seen as an activist that takes large positions in companies so it can influence management. Loeb is somewhat of the bad boy of the hedge fund world, and is known for his none-too-friendly e-mails and letters to company management. (The reader can do some Google searches to find an e-mail exchange with a potential hire that is especially entertaining.) He purchased (at the time) the most expensive Manhattan residence ever purchased ($45 million). The fund is named after a surf break in Malibu.

For 2008 the fund returned −38% and was trading at a discount of 50%. You can go to the web site and get all sorts of information in Third Point's monthly reports. As of this writing, the top five positions are Target Corp., Exco Resources, PHH Corp., Aspen Technology, and Teradata Corp.

Fund: BH Macro Ltd
   Manager: Brevan Howard Offshore
   Web site: www.bhmacro.com
   Location: London
   Listing: London Stock Exchange (LSE)
   Symbol: BHMG (Yahoo BHMG.L)
   Fund AUM ($): approximately $700 million
   Currency share classes: £, €, $

Brevan Howard was founded in 2002 by Alan Howard, and now employs nearly 400 people. Total assets under management surpass $20 billion, and returns have been approximately 14% per year with much less volatility than the S&P 500. The listed BH Macro fund invests all of its assets in the Brevan Howard Master Fund, and the underlying macro strategy served the fund well in 2008 with a 20% return. Despite this strong performance, the fund has traded at near 20% discounts to NAV.

Fund of Funds

This section details some of the largest funds of funds on the exchanges. Historically, these funds listed prior to the individual funds, are subsequently more numerous and have historically had more assets under management (although now they are near parity).

Fund: Dexion Absolute Ltd
   Manager: Harris Alternatives
   Web site: www.dexionabsolute.com, www.harrisalternatives.com
   Location: Chicago
   Listing: London (LSE)
   Symbol: DAB (Yahoo DAB.L)
   Fund AUM ($): approximately $1.0 billion
   Currency share classes: £, $, €, A$

Dexion is essentially the marketing arm of a number of funds (including Dexion Equity, Dexion Trading, and Dexion Alpha), and farms out the management of the funds to different managers. Dexion Absolute, the granddaddy of the listed FOF space, is managed by Harris Alternatives. Harris manages roughly $13 billion in its various funds.

The fund is managed in a similar manner as Harris's flagship fund Aurora. The investment objective is to generate consistent long-term capital appreciation with low volatility and little correlation with the general equity and bond markets through a portfolio having a diversified risk profile. Aurora has three main objectives: achieve steady capital appreciation, exhibit low volatility, and exhibit little correlation with the equity and fixed income markets. The fund has about 50 different managers spread across the following strategies:

Strategy	Allocation %
Long/Short Equity	34
Multistrategy	21
Portfolio Hedge	12
Global Macro	11
Long/Short Credit	11
Activist	11

This coincides nicely with Aurora's returns—since 1988 they are about 10% with volatility around 5%. Those are stock-like returns with a third of the volatility. The biggest drawdown was around 20%. More important, Aurora was up in 2000, 2001, and 2002—terrible years for the stock market. Some of Dexion's current holdings are in Palomino Fund, Lansdowne U.K. Equity Fund, Touradji Global Resources, and Ichan Fund.

Fund: Alternative Investment Strategies Ltd
    Manager: International Asset Management (part of ABN AMRO since 2006)
    Web site: www.aisinvest.com
    Location: London and New York City
    Listing: London (LSE)
    Symbol: AIS (Yahoo AIS.L)
    Fund AUM ($): approximately $200 million
    Currency share classes: £

Alternative Investment Strategies (AIS) was the first hedge fund to list in London, floating its offering in 1996. The managing firm was founded in 1989 by three former Drexel employees. Total assets under management are around $6 billion. A few of the fund's holdings are Karsh Capital, QVT Global, and Eminence Long Alpha. Since inception the fund has returned about 7.3% with volatility of 7.7%. AIS invests in between 20 and 40 funds with no single fund representing more than 10% of the gross assets. Roughly 40% of the fund is invested in long/short managers.

Fund: Goldman Sachs Dynamic Opportunities (GSDO)
    Manager: Goldman Sachs
    Web site: www.gs.com/gsdo
    Location: New York City
    Listing: London (LSE)
    Symbol: GSDO (Yahoo GSDO.L)
    Fund AUM ($): approximately $200 million
    Currency share classes: £, $, €

At the time of launch in 2006, GSDO was the largest IPO ever for a fund of hedge funds listed on the LSE. Targeting a relatively small group of managers at around 20, the fund has allocations to event driven (40%), equity long/short (26%), tactical trading (21%), and relative value (13%). GSDO has allocations to various funds including Tosca, Eton Park, Och–Ziff, Spinnaker, TPG-Axon, AQR, and D.E. Shaw. The fund has overcome its embarrassing investment in Amaranth and currently trades at a 25% discount to NAV.

Fund: Thames River Multi Hedge+
Manager: Thames River Capital
Web site: www.thamesriver.co.uk
Location: London
Listing: London (LSE)
Symbol: TRMU (Yahoo TRMU.L)
Fund AUM ($): approximately $300 million
Currency share classes: £, $, €

The Paulson example we cited earlier is a large reason Thames River returned 25% in 2007. Since inception in 2004 the fund has returned around 5% annually with volatility of 7%. Equity long/short is the largest allocation followed by macro, multistrategy, and credit. The fund invests in around 40 managers, and the largest allocations currently are GLG Emerging Markets, CQS Directional Opportunities, SOLA I, Bennelong Global, and BlueCrest Strategic.

Fund: Dexion Equity Alternative
Manager: K2 Advisors
Web site: www.dexionequity.com
Location: Stamford, London
Listing: London (LSE)
Symbol: DEA (Yahoo DEA.L)
Fund AUM ($): approximately $80 million
Currency share classes: £

K2 Advisors was founded in 1994 by William Douglas and David Saunders. Saunders is a Tiger Cub who was previously the head trader at Tiger Management. The firm has over $5 billion in assets under management. The listed fund has returned about 3% annualized since inception with volatility of around 6% (pegging the HFRI FOF Index) invested in roughly 30 funds.

Strategy	Allocation %
Long/Short Equity	53
Relative Value Arb	12
Specialist Credit	22
Alternative Strategies	3
Emerging Managers	3
Event Driven	7

For those investors interested in the sector, Table 6.8 offers a list of funds, the underlying manager, and their web sites.

Table 6.8 Fund Listing

Fund	Web Site	Manager
Multimanager/Multistrategy		
Absolute Return Trust	www.absolute-funds.com	Fauchier Partners
Aida	www.aidafund.com	Aida Capital
Alternative Inv. Strategies	www.aisinvest.com	Close Fund Services/International
Altin AG	www.altin.ch	Alternative Asset Advisors
CMA Global Hedge	www.cmaglobalhedge.com	Capital Management Advisors
Dexion Absolute	www.dexionabsolute.com	Dexion Capital/Harris Alternatives
Dexion Alpha Strategies	www.dexionalpha.com	Dexion Capital/RMF Investment
Dexion Equity Alternative	www.dexionequity.com	Dexion Capital/K2
Dexion Trading	www.dexiontrading.com	Dexion Capital/Permal Group
GS Dynamic Opportunities	www.gs.com/gsdo	Goldman Sachs Hedge Fund
Gottex Market Neutral	www.gottexfunds.com	Gottex Fund Management
HSBC European Absolute	www.hsbcabsolute.com	HSBC Management/HSBC
HSBC Global Absolute	www.hsbcabsolute.com	HSBC Management/HSBC
INVESCO Perp Select Hedge	www.invescoperpetual.co.uk/ipst	INVESCO/Fauchier Partners
KGR Absolute Return	www.kgrcapital.com	Kleinwort Benson (ChannelIslands)/
		KGR Capital
Opus Alternative Strategies	www.newfinancepartners.com	NewFinance Capital
PSolve Alternatives PCC	www.psolvealt.com	PSolve Alternative Investments
Tapestry	www.ramius.com	Kleinwort Benson (ChannelIslands)/
		Ramius HVB Partners
Thames River Hedge+	www.thamesriver.co.uk	Thames River Capital

(Continued)

129

Table 6.8 Fund Listing (*Continued*)

Fund	Web Site	Manager
Multimanager/Single–Strategy		
AcenciA Debt Strategies	www.acencia.com	Saltus/Sandalwood
F&C Event Driven	www.fandceventdriven.com	F&C Management/F&C Partners
FRM Credit Alpha	www.frmcredit.com	FRM Investment Management
Saltus Euro Debt Strategies	www.saltus.com	Saltus CI/Saltus Partners LLP
Signet Global Fixed Income	www.signetmanagement.com	Signet Capital Management
Single Manager/Fund of Funds		
Cazenove Absolute Equity	www.cazenovecapital.com	Cazenove Capital Management
Close AllBlue	www.closeallbluefund.com	BlueCrest Capital Management
Close Man Hedge	www.closemanhedgefund.com	Man Global Strategies
JPMorgan Progressive Multi-Strategy	www.jpmnprogressivemultistrategy.co.uk	JPMorgan Asset Management
Single Manager Hedge Funds		
BH Macro	www.bhmacro.com	Brevan Howard Offshore
Boussard & Gavaudan	www.bgholdingltd.com	Boussard & Gavaudan Asset
MW Tops	www.mwtops.eu	Marshall Wace
RAB Special Situations	www.rabspecialsituations.com	RAB Capital
Third Point Offshore	www.thirdpoint.com	Third Point LLC

Practical Considerations

There are a few things to consider before investing in these funds.

Because the funds trade on foreign exchanges, primarily in London, the investor needs to have a brokerage account that transacts in foreign securities. Most do, and Etrade and Interactive Brokers have simple user interfaces that allow investors to trade in foreign securities.

Most funds also have multiple share classes in different currencies, allowing the investors the benefit of hedging against adverse currency moves. U.S. investors want the dollar share class if available. Outside the top 10 funds, which are fairly liquid, the average fund has a 2% bid/ask spread. Investors must be careful and use limit orders when purchasing shares in these funds the same way they would trade small and micro-cap stocks here in the United States.

The biggest issues for the investor to consider revolve around the potential tax implications. While not certain, it is likely these foreign traded funds will be treated as Passive Foreign Investment Companies (PFICs). If they are, the investor has to make a mark-to-market election with the IRS, and then has to declare taxes on the gains and losses (and can only count losses against gains). If an investor has more losses than gains, the implications are unfortunate. The simplest course might be

Table 6.9 A Sample Portfolio Using Alternatives—Harvard and Yale with Alternatives (Rounded)

	Harvard 2007	Yale 2007	
Domestic Stocks	10%	10%	VTI
Foreign Developed Stocks	10	5	VEU
Foreign Emerging Stocks	10	10	VWO
Bonds	10	5	BVD
TIPS	5	–	TIP
Real Estate	10	15	VNQ
Commodities	15	15	DBC
Private Equity	10	20	PSP/PFP
Hedge Funds	20	20	XXX
Total	**100%**	**100%**	

for a prospective investor to invest in these funds using a tax-deferred account like an IRA. This is still a murky area for U.S. citizens, and the best course of action is to discuss this issue with your tax advisor.

There is the possibility that a fund or ETN could get around this problem with some clever financial engineering, but so far no one has launched a product.

Hedge funds can be invested in utilizing either U.S. mutual funds or foreign listed funds. Funds with high correlations to existing asset classes should be used as substitutions for existing allocations. Table 6.9 describes a sample allocation including private equity and hedge funds.

Summary

- Hedge fund managers pursue active strategies that attempt to generate alpha. Because of the fee structure, rewards for being a top manager are enormous.
- In 2007, there were over 10,000 funds managing about $2 trillion.
- Some benefits to investing in hedge funds include higher absolute and risk-adjusted returns, low correlation to traditional investments, and fewer constraints on the portfolio.
- Some potential drawbacks include accreditation requirements, lack of liquidity, manager selection, fraud, taxes, transparency, and top funds closed to new investors.
- Funds of funds can eliminate a lot of the portfolio construction and due diligence hassles but layer on extra fees.
- The United States is starting to see more hedge-like mutual funds and ETFs.
- The foreign listed hedge fund space is large and growing fast, currently around 50 funds with $20 billion in assets.
- An investor can access the foreign listed space, but caution is warranted due to legal and tax implications.

Part Three

ACTIVE MANAGEMENT

Chapter 7

Winning by Not Losing

The first rule is not to lose. The second rule is not to forget the first rule.
—WARREN BUFFETT

Many global asset classes in the twentieth century produced spectacular gains in wealth for individuals who bought and held those assets for generational-long holding periods. However, most of the common asset classes experienced painful drawdowns, and many investors can recall the 40% to 80% declines they faced in the aftermath of the internet bubble, and most recently the global equity market collapse in 2008. All of the G-7 countries have experienced at least one period where stocks lost 75% of their value. The unfortunate mathematics of a 75% decline require an investor to realize a 300% gain just to get back to even—the equivalent of compounding at 10% for 15 years. There have been more than 30 declines of greater than 20% since 1900 in the Dow, and 10 declines of greater than 40%.

Individuals invested in U.S. stocks in the late 1920s and early 1930s, German asset classes in the 1910s and 1940s, U.S. real estate in the mid-1950s, Japanese stocks in the late 1980s, emerging markets and commodities in the late 1990s, and global equities and commodities in 2008 (to name a few) would conclude that owning these assets was a decidedly poor course of action. Buying asset classes for the long run is a good idea if you are a Sequoia tree, a giant tortoise, or an endowment,[1] but individuals usually do not have a 20-year time frame to recover from large drawdowns.

That is the problem with investing; you have to accept some risk to receive the gains. First we will take a look at the inherent risks in various asset classes before highlighting a few of the behavioral biases that interfere with individuals' chances at investment success. With a good asset allocation based on the Policy Portfolios of the top endowments as a guide, we outline a very simple method to further reduce the risk in a portfolio. We then take a look at increasing returns with manageable levels of risk to attempt to approach the absolute level of endowment returns. But first—losing.

Losing Hurts

I am always thinking about losing money as opposed to making money.
—PAUL TUDOR JONES IN *MARKET WIZARDS*

What's with all the fascination about losing?

Modern portfolio theory tells you there is a trade-off for investing in assets—you get paid to assume risk. Figure 7.1 shows the five publicly traded asset classes we mentioned earlier, and their returns since 1973 (calendar year returns ending December 31). While they took different routes to get there, most all of the asset classes finished with similar returns. The exception was bonds that trailed the other asset classes, which is to be expected.

Table 7.1 shows the actual numbers, and while there are some pretty nice returns, there are some large drawdowns.[2] With the exception of U.S. government bonds that declined almost 20%, the other four asset classes had drawdowns around 50%. And if an investor were to take the data back further, those drawdowns can only get bigger.[3] U.S. equities experienced a roughly 80% decline following the 1929 crash.

---

[1] Thanks to Greg Morris for the analogy.
[2] While the endowments only report annual return numbers, we use annualized monthly volatility figures for this chapter which will differ slightly from the annual figures.
[3] Higher resolution daily data will increase the drawdowns as well.

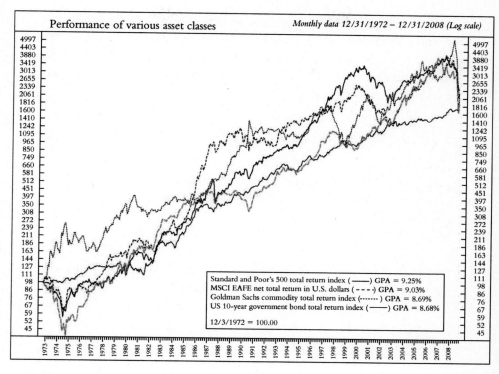

Figure 7.1 Performance of Various Asset Classes
© Copyright 2008 Ned Davis Research, Inc.

Table 7.1 Maximum Drawdowns, 1973–2008

	U.S. Stocks	Foreign Stocks	10 YR	Commod	Real Estate
Annualized Return	9.26%	9.04%	8.69%	8.73%	8.54%
Volatility	15.54%	17.18%	9.06%	17.04%	17.06%
Sharpe 6%	0.21	0.18	0.30	0.16	0.15
Maximum Drawdown	−44.73%	−49.21%	−18.79%	−62.16%	−58.78%
Best Year	37.58%	69.94%	44.28%	74.96%	48.97%
Worst Year	−36.77%	−43.06%	−7.51%	−46.49%	−42.23%

There is nothing worse than watching a portfolio experience a long and painful decline. As we examined earlier, digging a hole that big is hard to recover from. Human biases make the returns to individuals in these asset classes even worse than stated previously. Next we take a look at a few of the more common biases.

You Are Your Own Worst Enemy

Investing is not a game where the guy with the 160 IQ beats the guy with the 130 IQ. . . . Once you have ordinary intelligence, what you need is the temperament to control the urges that get other people into trouble in investing.

—WARREN BUFFETT

Millions of years of evolution by natural selection equipped humans to be quite good at survival, but quite bad at timing trades of Google and oil futures. We display all sorts of behavioral biases that muck up our chances at investment success. Remember piling into the dotcoms in the late 1990s only to sell them in 2003? You're not alone; investors love to herd into an asset class at the top and sell at the bottom. Stock funds accounted for 99% and 123% of mutual fund flows in 1999 and 2000, respectively. You read that right, people were selling off their other holdings to plow money into stocks. And reported mutual fund returns are almost always higher than individual investor returns due to this poor timing.

From 1973–2002 NASDAQ stocks gained 9.6% per year, but because most investors pumped in money from 1998—to 2000, the typical dollar invested earned only 4.3% a year (Dichev, 2007). Tale after tale of irrationality in financial markets can be found in Charles Mackay's *Extraordinary Popular Delusions and the Madness of Crowds*, and Charles Kindleberger's *Manias, Panics, and Crashes.*[4]

The field known as behavioral finance was founded in the 1970s to study these phenomena as applied to financial markets. Much of the early work was done by professors Amos Tversky and Daniel

---

[4]For a good overview of behavioral biases check out Jason Zweig's book, *Your Money and Your Brain* and the reading list for more examples.

Kahneman. One of their findings was that people are very reluctant to sell their losers (called prospect theory). While there are dozens of documented ways in which people are irrational when it comes to money, a few of the more insidious biases include:

- **Overconfidence**—82% of drivers say they are in the top 30% of drivers, and 80% of students think they will finish in the top half of their class (Tilson, 2005).
- **Information overload**—More information often decreases accuracy of predictions, all the while increasing confidence in those predictions. Paul Andreassen, a psychologist formerly at Harvard University, conducted a series of laboratory experiments in the 1980s to see how investors respond to news. He found that people who pay close attention to news updates actually earn lower returns by excessively trading than people who seldom follow the news.
- **Herding**—From 1987 through 2007, the S&P returned more than 10% per year. However, the average investor in a stock mutual fund earned only 4.48%. That means that over these past 20 years, the average equity mutual fund investor would have barely kept up with inflation (Dalbar, 2008). This underperformance is mainly because investors exhibit poor market timing, buying at the top and selling at the bottom.
- **Avoiding losses**—People feel pain of loss twice as much as they derive pleasure from an equal gain (Tversky, 1979). More than 40 years ago Philip Fisher wrote in *Common Stocks and Uncommon Profits*, "There is a complicating factor that makes the handling of investment mistakes more difficult. This is the ego in each of us. None of us likes to admit to himself that he has been wrong. . . . More money has probably been lost by investors holding a stock they really did not want until they could 'at least come out even' than from any other single reason."
- **Anchoring**—During normal decision making, individuals anchor (or overly rely on) specific information or a specific value and then adjust to that value. Once the anchor is set, there is a bias toward that value. Warren Buffett laments: "When I bought something at X and it went up to X and 1/8th, I sometimes stopped buying, perhaps hoping it would come back down. We've missed billions when I've gotten anchored. I cost us about $10 billion [by not buying enough

Wal-Mart]. I set out to buy 100 million shares, presplit, at $23. We bought a little and it moved up a bit and I thought it might come back a bit—who knows? That thumb-sucking, the reluctance to pay a little more, cost us a lot" (2004 Berkshire Hathaway annual meeting).

Of course, this information is not only valuable for figuring out our own biases; other people's mistakes leave the door open for you to soak up some of that elusive alpha we talked about earlier. Remember, as far as excess returns (alpha) are concerned, for someone to gain someone else has to lose. People consistently make the same mistakes that are hardwired into their brains and do so over and over again.

A very simple quantitative approach can avoid all the behavioral biases humans make in their investment decision making process, and help you avoid errors like piling into CMGI in early 2000 and selling it in 2003.

More important, you will not constantly be asking the question: What do I do?

We have reviewed that asset classes are risky and experience large and painful drawdowns. The first step in crafting an endowment style portfolio has been to follow the strategic asset allocation of the endowments to create a balanced Policy Portfolio involving numerous asset classes.

To further reduce the risk in a portfolio we will examine a simple system and show why market timing is not a dirty phrase (the institutions like to call it by the more sophisticated name of *tactical asset allocation*). We will take a look at a simple, easy-to-follow, quantitative system for market timing that will help to achieve stock-like returns with bond-like volatility and drawdown. Let's get started.

Playing Defense

> *A loss never bothers me after I take it. I forget it overnight. But being wrong—not taking the loss—that is what does damage to the pocketbook and to the soul.*
>
> —JESSIE LIVERMORE IN *REMINISCENCES OF*
> *A STOCK OPERATOR* BY EDWIN LEFÈVRE

So, is there a way to avoid these long bear markets and losses?

This section could just as easily be called risk management. Most of this chapter is based on a paper Mebane Faber published in *The*

Journal of Wealth Management in 2007 titled, "A Quantitative Approach to Tactical Asset Allocation." The paper could have been named "A Quantitative Approach to Risk Management." People react way too emotionally to the phrase "market timing" for that to be the title, but in reality they are all the same thing.

The application of a trend following methodology to financial markets is not a new endeavor, and an entire book by Michael Covel (2005) has been written on the subject. The rules and criteria of a trend following strategy are incredibly varied and unique, but at the end of the day they all attempt to do the same thing: catch the majority of a positive move in an asset class. In essence, we're talking about momentum.[5]

The Quantitative System

There are a few criteria that are necessary for this to be a simple model that investors can follow and mechanical enough to remove the emotions involved in subjective decision making. They are:

1. Simple, purely mechanical logic.
2. The same model and parameters for every asset class.
3. Price-based only.

Moving-average-based trading systems are the simplest and most popular trend following systems.[6] For those unfamiliar with moving averages, they are simply a way to reduce noise. Figure 7.2 is an example showing the S&P 500 back to 1990 along with a 10-month simple moving average.

The most often cited long-term measure of trend in the technical analysis community is the 200-day simple moving average (SMA). In his book *Stocks for the Long Run,* Jeremy Siegel (2006) investigates the use of the 200-day SMA in timing the Dow Jones Industrial Average (DJIA) from 1886–2006. His test bought the DJIA when it closed

---

[5]Instead of offering a lengthy review of momentum and trend following in this chapter, we will post a bibliography including links to papers and literature on the book web site (www.theivyportfolio.com). Appendix A covers a very short history of the momentum literature.

[6]Taylor and Allen (1992) and Lui and Mole (1998).

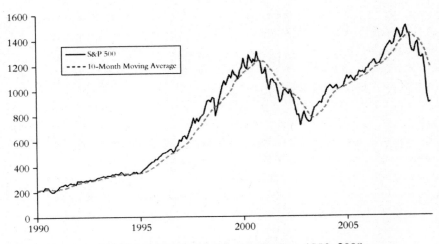

Figure 7.2   S&P 500 and 10-Month Moving Average 1990–2008

at least 1% above the 200-day moving average, and sold the DJIA and invested in Treasury bills when it closed at least 1% below the 200-day moving average.[5]

He concludes that market timing improves the absolute and risk-adjusted returns over a buy-and-hold of the DJIA. Likewise, when all transaction costs are included (taxes, bid-ask spread, commissions), the risk-adjusted return is still higher when employing market timing, though timing falls short on an absolute return measure. When applied to the NASDAQ Composite since 1972, the market timing system thoroughly outperforms the buy-and-hold, both on an absolute and risk-adjusted basis. Siegel finds that the timing model outperforms buy-and-hold by over 4% per year from 1972–2006 even when accounting for all costs—and with 25% less volatility. Unfortunately, Siegel does not report drawdown figures, which would have shown the superiority of the timing model even more. (Note: Siegel's system is twice as active as the system presented in this chapter, thus increasing the transaction costs.)

We use the monthly equivalent of Siegel's 200-day SMA—the 10-month SMA. Because we were privy to Siegel's results before conducting the test, this query on U.S. stocks should be seen as in-sample.

(That just means we already got a peek at the data. Out-of-sample testing is a better indicator of a system's robustness).[7]

The system is as follows:

Buy Rule: Buy when monthly price > 10-month SMA.
Sell Rule: Sell and move to cash when monthly price < 10-month SMA.

(For those unfamiliar with moving averages, stockcharts.com is a good web site that allows users to graph moving averages on asset classes and funds. More important, they account for dividends in their total return calculations.)

Beyond that, keep in mind:

- All entry and exit prices are on the day of the signal at the close. The model is only updated once a month on the last day of the month. Anything going on during the rest of the month is ignored.
- All data series are total return series including dividends, updated monthly.
- Cash returns are estimated with 90-day Treasury bills, and margin rates (for leveraged models to be discussed later) are estimated with the broker call rate.
- Taxes, commissions, and slippage are excluded (see "practical considerations" section later in the chapter).

That's it. The rules are simple, but for some people they are hard to follow. Why is that? For the same reason people have a hard time dieting, or training for marathons, or cleaning out the garage: self control and discipline.

The Quantitative System in Action

To demonstrate the logic and characteristics of the timing system, we test the S&P 500 back to 1900. Table 7.2 presents the yearly returns

---

[7]It is possible that Siegel already optimized the moving average by looking back over the period in which it is then tested. Faber's paper applied the approach out-of-sample to over 20 additional markets to test for validity and alleviate fears of data snooping.

Table 7.2   S&P 500 Total Returns vs. Timing Total
Returns (1900–2008)

	S&P 500	Timing
Annualized Return	9.21%	10.45%
Volatility	17.87%	12.02%
Sharpe 4%	0.29	0.54
Maximum Drawdown	−83.66%	−50.31%
Best Year	52.88%	52.40%
Worst Year	−43.86%	−26.87%

Total return series is provided by Global Financial Data, Inc. and results
pre-1971 are constructed by Global Financial Data, Inc. Data from
1900–1971 uses the S&P Composite Price Index and dividend yields
supplied by Cowles Commission and from S&P itself.

for U.S. stocks (S&P 500) and the timing method for the past 100+
years. A cursory glance at the results reveals that the timing solution
improved compounded return, while reducing risk (standard deviation,
drawdown, worst year), all while being invested in the market approximately 70% of the time, and making less than one round trip trade
per year.

The timing system achieves these superior results while underperforming the index in roughly 40% of the years since 1900. One of the
reasons for the overall outperformance is the lower volatility of the timing system, due to high volatility diminishing compound (geometric)
returns. This fact can be illustrated by comparing average returns with
compounded returns (or the returns an investor would actually realize).
The average return for the S&P 500 since 1900 was 11.20%, while timing the S&P 500 returned 11.49%. However, the compounded returns
for the two are 9.21% and 10.45%, respectively. Notice that the buy-
and-hold index takes a 199 basis point hit from the effects of volatility,
while timing suffers a smaller, 104 basis point decline. Ed Easterling has
a good discussion of these "volatility gremlins" in John Mauldin's book,
Just One Thing (2006).

From Figure 7.3, it is apparent that the timing is superior over the
past century (logarithmic scale), largely avoiding the significant bear
markets of the 1930s and 2000s. Timing would not have left the investor

completely unscathed from the late 1920s and early 1930s bear market, but it would have reduced the drawdown from a catastrophic 83.66% to 44.04%. People often remark that the difference doesn't look that substantial on this chart, but that is because it is a logarithmic chart. Logarithmic charts should always be used when viewing charts over longer time periods because they equalize percentage changes across time frames and price levels.

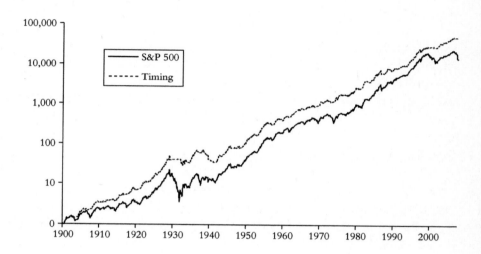

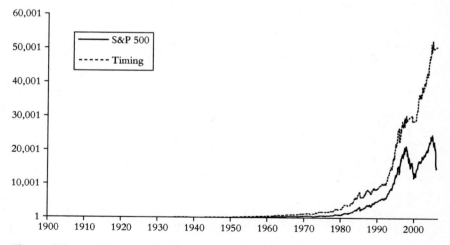

Figure 7.3 S&P 500 Performance from 1900 to 2008

The second nonlogarithmic chart looks like one of those shady newspaper ads that say something like, "Follow my uranium picks and you could make 9,472%!!" This difference in charts goes to illustrate another point: Even small differences in returns, when compounded over long periods, result in large differences in final value. In this case the investor using the timing model would have ended up with over twice the final portfolio amount. A hypothetical $100 invested with a buy-and-hold approach in 1900 would be worth nearly $1.5 million by 2008, while the same $100 utilizing the timing method would be worth $5 million.

Examining the most recent 15 years, a few features of the timing model become evident. Figure 7.4 is charted on a nonlog scale to detail the differences in the two equity curves. First, a trend following model will underperform buy-and-hold during a roaring bull market similar to the U.S. equity markets in the 1990s. The ability of the timing model to add value needs to be recognized over the course of an entire business cycle, however.

The second feature is that the timing model will not participate in a lengthy and protracted bear market. The timing model exits the long investment in October of 2000, thus avoiding two of the three consecutive years of losses, and the 44.73% drawdown buy-and-hold investors experienced with a more mild 16.52%. Similarly, the timing

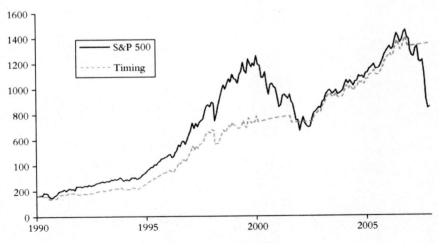

Figure 7.4   S&P 500 Performance from 1990 to 2008

model would have moved to cash at the end of 2007, thus avoiding the steep stock market drop in 2008.

Table 7.3 presents the top 10 worst years for the S&P 500 for the past century, and the corresponding returns for the timing system. It is immediately obvious that the two do not move in lockstep. In fact, the correlation between negative years on the S&P 500 and the timing model is approximately −.38, while the correlation for all years is approximately 0.81.

Disadvantages of Market Timing

Now that we have gone through an example with one asset class to highlight the benefits of the system, below are three potential downsides.

1. Market timing can underperform buy-and-hold in a strong bull market.
2. Market timing requires resolve, discipline, and commitment similar to what's needed to lose weight or train for a marathon.
3. You can have multiple losing trades in a row.

Table 7.3 S&P 10 Worst Years versus Timing

	S&P 500	**Timing**
1931	−43.86%	1.41%
2008	−36.77	1.33
1937	−35.26	−7.65
1907	−29.61	−0.09
1974	−26.47	8.16
1917	−25.26	−3.02
1930	−25.26	2.51
2002	−22.10	−4.62
1920	−19.69	−4.80
1973	−14.69	−15.36

Source: Global Financial Data.

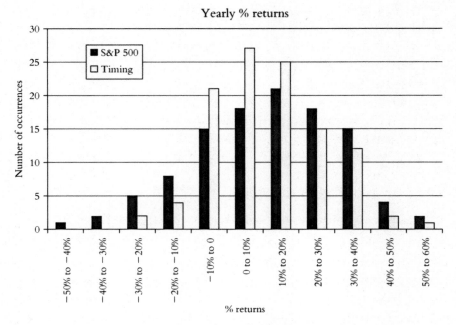

Figure 7.5 Yearly Percentage Returns, S&P 500 vs. Timing

Figure 7.5 gives a good pictorial description of the results of the trend following system applied to the S&P 500. The timing system has fewer occurrences of both large gains and large losses, with correspondingly higher occurrences of small gains and losses. (This is an example of reducing the fat tails of a distribution. Nassim Taleb devotes an entire book to fat tails in his book *The Black Swan*.) Essentially the system is a model that signals when an investor should be long a riskier asset class with potential upside and when to be out and sitting in cash. It is this move to a lower volatility asset class (cash) that drops the overall risk and drawdown of the portfolio.

It is possible that Siegel (or others) have optimized the moving average by looking back over the period tested. As a check against optimization, and to show that using the 10-month SMA is not a unique solution, Figures 7.6 to 7.9 present the stability of using various parameters. Calculation periods will perform differently in the future as

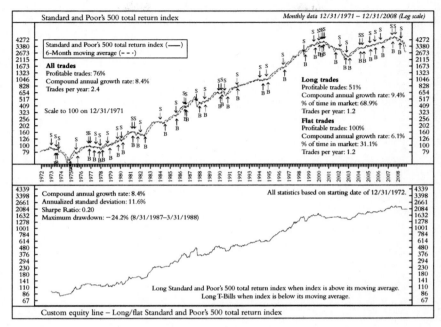

Figure 7.6 S&P 500 and 6-Month Moving Average Timing Model
© Copyright 2008 Ned Davis Research, Inc.

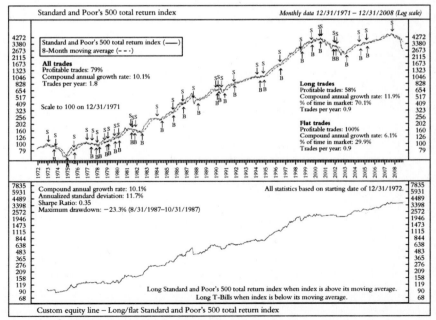

Figure 7.7 S&P 500 and 8-Month Moving Average Timing Model
© Copyright 2008 Ned Davis Research, Inc.

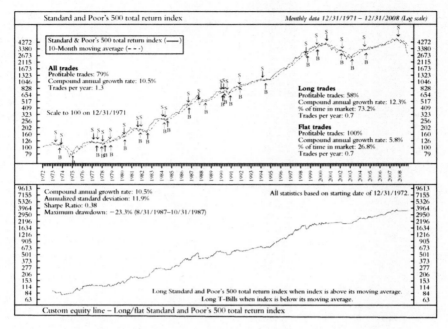

Figure 7.8   S&P 500 and 10-Month Moving Average Timing Model
© Copyright 2008 Ned Davis Research, Inc.

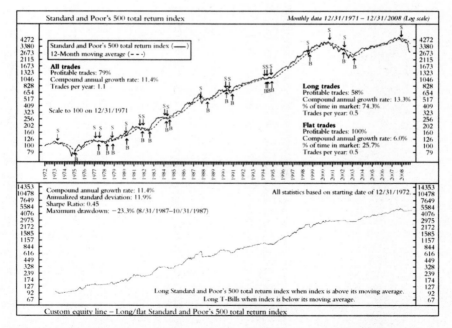

Figure 7.9   S&P 500 and 12-Month Moving Average Timing Model
© Copyright 2008 Ned Davis Research, Inc.

cyclical and secular forces drive the return series, but all of the parameters seem to work similarly for a long-term trend following application.

The 10-month SMA is not the optimum parameter for any of the statistics, but it is evident that there is very broad parameter stability across the various moving average lengths.

Out-of-Sample Testing and Systematic Tactical Asset Allocation

To address the possibility of data snooping, the quantitative model is tested out-of-sample on markets other than the S&P 500. The results of a stable model should translate to all asset classes.

In addition to the S&P 500, the same four asset classes were chosen including foreign stocks (MSCI EAFE), U.S. bonds (10-year Treasuries), commodities (GSCI), and real estate (NAREIT). Table 7.4 presents the results for each asset class, and the respective timing results from 1973–2008. Figures 7.10 through 7.13 illustrate the equity curves for the timing model on each asset class.

While timing model returns are approximately the same as buy-and-hold for each asset class (although higher in all five), risk was reduced in every case across volatility and maximum drawdown. Better yet, the results and trading statistics were consistent across the five asset classes.

The average winning trade was seven times larger than the average losing trade, and the length in winners was six times larger than the length of losing trades. Percent winning trades across the five asset classes was at an uncharacteristically high (for trend following systems) 50%.

Given the ability of this very simple market timing rule to add value to various asset classes, it is instructive to examine how the returns would look in the context of an investor's portfolio. The timing model treats each asset class independently—it is either long the asset class or in cash with its 20% allocation of the funds.

Table 7.5 presents the results for the buy-and-hold portfolio of the five asset classes equal-weighted (Ivy) versus the timing portfolio with the same five asset classes. The Ivy Portfolio returns are quite respectable on a stand-alone basis and present evidence of the benefits of diversification. The timing results in a reduction in volatility to single-digit levels,

Table 7.4   Timing Results (1973–2008)

	S&P 500	Timing
Annualized Return	9.26%	10.60%
Volatility	15.55%	11.90%
Sharpe	0.21	0.39
Max Drawdown	−44.73%	−23.26%
	EAFE	**Timing**
Annualized Return	9.04%	11.10%
Volatility	17.18%	12.47%
Sharpe	0.18	0.41
Max Drawdown	−49.21%	−23.16%
	10 Year	**Timing**
Annualized Return	8.69%	8.79%
Volatility	9.06%	7.48%
Sharpe	0.30	0.37
Max Drawdown	−18.79%	−11.20%
	GSCI	**Timing**
Annualized Return	8.73%	11.16%
Volatility	20.48%	17.04%
Sharpe	0.13	0.30
Max Drawdown	−62.16%	−37.83%
	NAREIT	**Timing**
Annualized Return	8.54%	11.74%
Volatility	17.06%	11.55%
Sharpe	0.15	0.50
Max Drawdown	−58.78%	−20.90%

as well as single-digit drawdown. The investor would not have experienced a down year since inception in 1973. The model rebalances monthly, and Figures 7.14 to 7.16 show the returns for monthly and yearly rebalancing.

The results for 2006–2008 are out of sample since the model was published with results up to 2005 in Faber's paper. (Using the annual standard deviation of returns for volatility rather than annualized monthly produces an even higher Sharpe Ratio difference.)

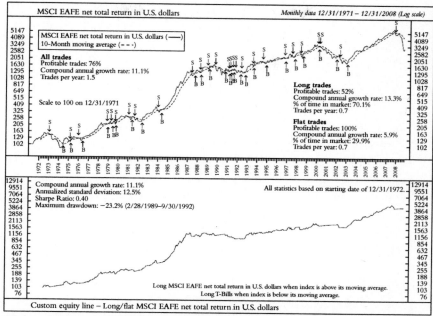

Figure 7.10   MSCI EAFE and 10-Month Moving Average Timing Model
© Copyright 2008 Ned Davis Research, Inc.

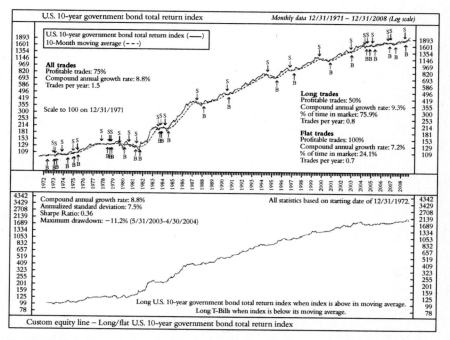

Figure 7.11   U.S. 10-Year Government Bond and 10-Month Moving Average
Timing Model
© Copyright 2008 Ned Davis Research, Inc.

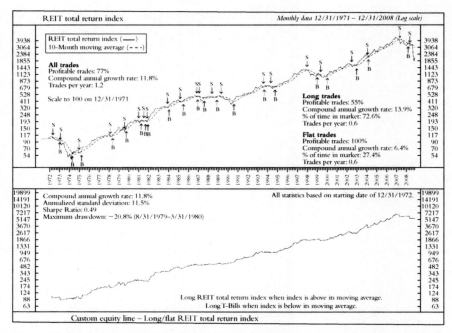

Figure 7.12 REIT and 10-Month Moving Average Timing Model
© Copyright 2008 Ned Davis Research, Inc.

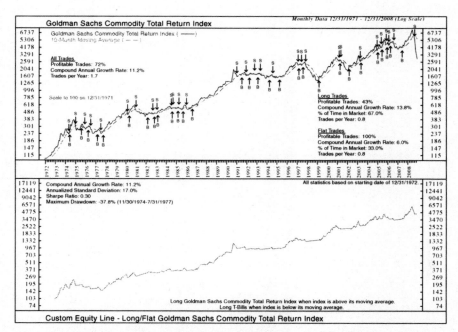

Figure 7.13 GSCI and 10-Month Moving Average Timing Model
© Copyright 2008 Ned Davis Research, Inc.

Table 7.5 The Ivy Portfolio versus Timing (1973–2008), Fiscal Year Ending June 30th

	Ivy Portfolio	Timing	Leveraged Timing
1973	1.03%	7.39%	6.71%
1974	−11.80	12.07	15.59
1975	20.16	1.46	−3.87
1976	15.04	16.01	26.95
1977	8.24	7.20	8.49
1978	13.65	11.88	15.25
1979	17.89	14.65	16.29
1980	18.95	12.91	10.02
1981	−3.34	4.80	−5.40
1982	21.34	22.06	32.47
1983	17.97	15.77	21.77
1984	9.43	6.98	3.35
1985	26.58	26.20	46.12
1986	25.50	21.54	36.39
1987	8.53	11.63	15.39
1988	18.46	11.74	15.37
1989	19.25	18.12	27.02
1990	−1.10	4.94	1.64
1991	18.19	6.34	5.47
1992	3.88	4.72	4.80
1993	11.90	12.82	21.62
1994	1.76	2.43	−0.02
1995	22.74	21.73	37.90
1996	19.32	19.26	32.73
1997	9.96	9.94	12.55
1998	−0.49	7.38	8.92
1999	14.16	13.05	20.83
2000	12.73	13.78	20.50
2001	−9.74	3.21	2.76
2002	2.09	3.39	4.50
2003	25.70	20.53	41.50
2004	17.44	15.06	28.20
2005	11.74	8.20	11.26
2006	12.07	14.16	22.53
2007	8.06	9.49	12.93
2008	−30.09%	−0.59	−2.83
Annualized Return	9.77%	11.27%	15.27%
Volatility	9.73%	6.87%	13.78%
Sharpe	0.39	0.77	0.67
Maximum Drawdown	−35.98%	−9.53%	−21.91%
Best Year	26.58%	26.20%	46.12%
Worst Year	−30.09%	−0.59%	−5.40%

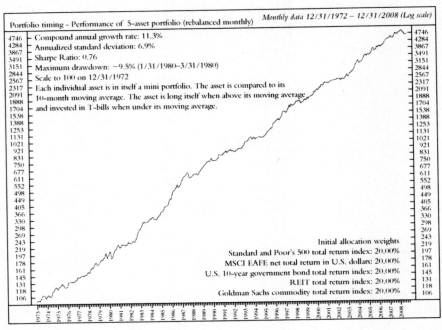

Figure 7.14   10-Month Moving Average Timing Model on the Ivy Portfolio, Rebalanced Monthly

© Copyright 2008 Ned Davis Research, Inc.

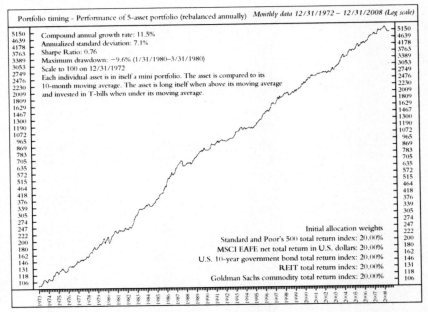

Figure 7.15   10-Month Moving Average Timing Model on the Ivy Portfolio, Rebalanced Yearly

© Copyright 2008 Ned Davis Research, Inc.

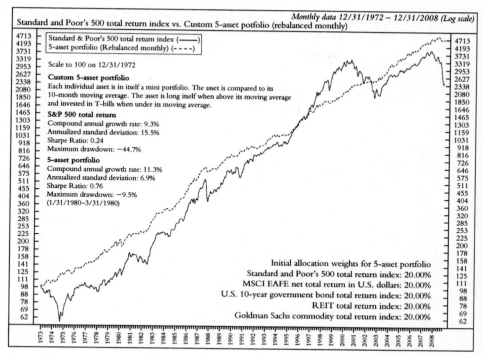

Figure 7.16 10-Month Moving Average Timing Model on the Ivy Portfolio vs. the S&P 500, Rebalanced Monthly
© Copyright 2008 Ned Davis Research, Inc.

Table 7.6 Average Number of Positions 1973–2008

Number of Positions	% Invested	Number of Months	Percentage of Months
0 (all cash)	0%	5	1.16%
1	20	20	4.63%
2	40	52	12.04%
3	60	94	21.76%
4	80	164	37.96%
5	100	97	22.45%
Total		**432**	**100.00%**

Table 7.6 illustrates the percentage of months in which various numbers of assets were held. It is evident that the system keeps the investor 60% to 100% invested the vast majority of the time.

Extensions

There are a number of potential improvements one can make to the timing model, including:

- **Shorting**—A long/short approach to the timing model produces returns around 9% with volatility of 8% and drawdowns of 16.3%. While the returns are worse than long/flat, the correlation to a buy and hold portfolio moves to zero. An equity curve is in the appendix.
- **More asset classes**—Our research has shown that further dividing up an index can create additional reductions in volatility. For example, instead of timing the MSCI EAFE, trade the components Japan, U.K., Germany, Switzerland, and so on.
- **Different asset classes**—Our research has shown that adding some slices that have historically outperformed can make sense, like small caps and value stocks.
- **No bonds**—Because the model is in cash roughly 30% of the time, the investor already has an allocation to bonds (T-bills). Our research has shown that excluding bonds can increase returns while only marginally increasing volatility and drawdown.
- **High volatility asset classes**—Our research has shown that the highest volatility asset classes respond the best to the timing model. Adding emerging market bonds, junk bonds, small cap emerging market stocks, and so on could make sense.

Some people are not interested in risk reduction but rather higher returns. An obvious extension of this approach is to apply leverage to generate excess returns to the nonleveraged portfolio. The biggest difficulty with a leveraged portfolio for the individual investor is implementation. Margin fees are onerous at many online brokerages. If your margin rates are much higher than the rates you receive on cash, then using leverage is not a good option.[8]

---

[8]Interactive Brokers has consistently reasonable margin rates even though we do not use them as a brokerage.

Additionally, the leveraged ETFs do not behave like a two times leveraged index (they are rebalanced daily), introducing tracking error and potentially subpar performance. However, for those with low borrowing costs, leveraging the portfolio 100% could increase returns to the 15% range with increased volatility, and drawdowns doubling to around 20%. We included an equity curve in Appendix B for this approach. The Sharpe Ratio takes a small hit due to the difference in borrowing costs exceeding the risk free rate.

There is a simpler method for the investor who does not want to use leverage and margin, and next we examine a rotation system.

A Rotation System

The second most asked question is: "What about going all in? Instead of going to cash, you equal-weight all of the asset classes on a buy?"

The problem here is the loss of diversification benefits. In the rare case when only one asset class is on a buy signal, the portfolio is exposed to unnecessary risk. Additionally the portfolio will have much higher turnover.

The timing model presented earlier compares an asset class to itself— is real estate going up or down? Another method is a relative strength (or cross-market momentum) system, which compares assets to each other— is real estate going up more than bonds? This can also be called a rotation system as you are rotating into what is performing best over a given time period. Many people have researched such systems over 50 years ago and they have continued to work decades after publication.

We explore a similar system here. The system uses the same five asset classes as before. Each month, the 3-, 6-, and 12-month total returns are recorded for each asset class and then averaged. The actual time frame selected does not matter much as the 3-, 6-, and 12-month time frames all produce similar results. We prefer using all three because it picks the asset classes that are outperforming in numerous time frames.

The investor then simply invests in the top X asset classes for the following month. For example, at the end of 2007 the order of returns from best to worst was commodities, foreign stocks, bonds, U.S. stocks, and real estate. The portfolio for the next month in 2008 would be in that same order.

Table 7.7 Rotation Strategies (1973–2008)

	Ivy Portfolio	Top 1	Top 2	Top 3
Annualized Return	9.77%	17.55%	16.42%	13.94%
Volatility	9.73%	18.62%	12.39%	10.84%
Sharpe	0.39	0.62	0.84	0.73
Maximum Drawdown	−35.98%	−33.90%	−27.52%	−32.60%

In Table 7.7 we show the results of taking the top one, two, and three asset classes, updated monthly, based on the average of the rolling 3-, 6-, and 12-month total returns. (Top 1 means you just take the top asset class each month. Top 2 means you select the top two asset classes each month and put 50% of the portfolio in each, Top 3 is the top three assets with 33% in each, etc.). Ivy Portfolio is the same as earlier with 20% in each asset class. All are rebalanced monthly.

While simply taking the top-performing asset class may seem like a good idea because it returns over 17% a year, in reality it is not. Investing 100% of your portfolio in only one asset class leaves the investor exposed to market shocks, and consequently the turnover, volatility, and drawdowns are higher for a single asset class. A better idea would be to invest in the top two or three asset classes each month which amounts to approximately half of the investable universe.

For similar risk as buy-and-hold, taking the top three positions outperforms by over 4% per year, with a similar Sharpe Ratio as the timing model. We expect 0.80 to be a consistent target for a momentum approach to tactical asset allocation regardless of the exact strategy employed. This strategy outperforms the buy-and-hold Ivy Portfolio about 70% of the years, and 10 of the past 15 years. So much for momentum no longer working!

Practical Considerations and Taxes

There are a few practical considerations an investor must analyze before implementing these models for real-world applicability—namely management fees, taxes, commissions, and slippage. Management fees should be identical for the buy-and-hold and timing models, and will vary depending on the instruments used for investing. 0.1% to 0.8% is a fair estimate for these fees using ETFs and no-load mutual funds.

Commissions should be a minimal factor due to the low turnover of the models. For the timing model, on average, the investor would be making three to four round-trip trades per year for the entire portfolio, and less than one round-trip trade per asset class per year (that is about 70% turnover). The top three rotation system results in a little higher turnover of around 100%.

Slippage, resulting from paying large bid-ask spreads, likewise should be near negligible, as there are numerous mutual funds (zero slippage) as well as liquid ETFs an investor can choose from.

Taxes, on the other hand, are a very real consideration. Many institutional investors such as endowments and pension funds enjoy tax-exempt status. The obvious solution for individuals is to trade the system in a tax-deferred account such as an IRA or 401(k). Due to the various capital gains rates for different investors (as well as varying tax rates across time and by state) it is difficult to estimate the hit an investor would suffer from trading this system in a taxable account.

Most investors trade or rebalance their holding periodically—introducing some turnover to the portfolio—and it is reasonable to assume a normal turnover of approximately 20%. The timing system has a turnover of almost 70%. Gannon and Blum (2006) presented after-tax returns for individuals invested in the S&P 500 since 1961 in the highest tax bracket. After-tax returns to investors with 20% turnover would have fallen to 6.72% from a pre-tax return of 10.62%. They estimate that an increase in turnover from 20% to 70% would have resulted in less than an additional 50 basis point hit to performance to 6.27%. There is a bright note for those who have to trade this model in a taxable account. The nature of the system results in a high number of short-term capital losses, and a large percentage of long-term capital gains. (The rotation system would take a slightly larger hit due to the higher turnover.)

Figure 7.17 depicts the distribution for all the timing model trades for the five individual asset classes since 1973. This should help reduce the tax burden for the investor. Interestingly enough, one of the longest

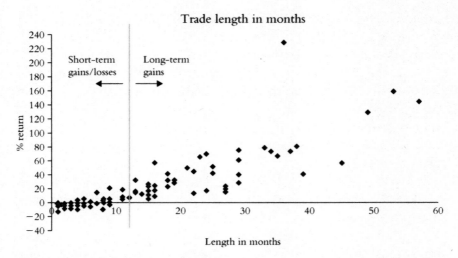

Figure 7.17　Trade Distribution

trades ever recently exited—the MSCI EAFE—was purchased in May of 2003 and held until early 2008 for more than a double.

Discipline

I always say that you could publish my trading rules in the newspaper and no one would follow them. The key is consistency and discipline. Almost anybody can make up a list of rules that are 80% as good as what we taught our people. What they couldn't do is give them the confidence to stick to those rules even when things are going bad.

　　　　　　　　　　　　　　　　　　　　　　—RICHARD DENNIS

The biggest question for someone following a quantitative system is: "Can I follow it?" It is not as easy as it sounds. These questions apply equally to strategic asset allocation and rebalancing as they do to market timing. Here are six questions from Merriman Capital to help you determine if you have what it takes.

1. Do you have the necessary perseverance?
2. Are you independent and self-assured enough to resist temptation to constantly look over your shoulder to see how someone else is doing?

3. Can you accept that your portfolio will underperform the market?
4. Can you accept that your timing system will be imperfect?
5. Can you ignore the mass media?
6. Are you decisive?

Before ending the chapter we wanted to offer one quick diversion lest you think we bow at the altar of momentum only.

Blood in the Streets
The time to buy is when blood is running in the streets.
—BARON ROTHSCHILD

Having just extolled the virtues of a trend following system, how about examining the opposite behavior, mean reversion? Mean reversion is a process where prices return to their average.

An economics book written by Davidson and Rees-Mogg entitled *Blood in the Streets: Investment Profits in a World Gone Mad* credits Baron Rothschild with the above quotation. The crucial question is whether it is possible for the investor to know when exactly "blood is running in the streets" (not literally we hope).

Would a percentage decline be a good measure? What about low P/E ratios or investor sentiment? People love trying to call market bottoms. With all of the financial noise and misinformation available at a keystroke, it is difficult for the modern investor to make sound and nonemotional investment decisions and avoid catching a falling knife.

A researcher could simply flip the cross market momentum system mentioned previously to examine the results of investing in the worst performing asset classes. The drawback of this method is that it fails to capture the emotions inherent in *losing money*. Simply taking the worst performing asset classes could mean investing in asset classes that had positive performance less than the top performing asset classes. Investing in an asset

(Continued)

Blood in the Streets (*Continued*)

class that returned 10% versus other assets returning 12% is far easier to do than investing in an asset class that was down 20% each of the prior two years.

Were you buying stocks in 2003? Very likely you were not watching CNBC and you probably quit opening and reading your brokerage statements.

Will the market structures examined continue in the future? The answer is yes as long as the behavioral biases inherent in investor decision making continue, and as long as humans continue to experience the emotions of greed and fear.

See Tables 7.8 and 7.9. The first looks at yearly returns for five stock markets from 1903 to 2007: U.S., U.K., Germany, France, and Australia.[9] The average return was about 13%, and the median return was 10.65%. About 70% of all years were positive.

In Table 7.8 we examine what happens when you invest for a year after losing money in two or three consecutive years. For example, three down years in a row occurred in 2003 in the United States for stocks after down years in 2000, 2001, and 2002.

A down year two years in a row increases average returns about 4% but only happens about 10% of the time. Three negative years in a row result in median returns of about 30% a year. While this occurs somewhat infrequently, the results are very positive.

Extending the test to other asset classes shows similar results. When the past few years were negative, it is a good time to be in an asset class. Stocks in 1975 and 2003, commodities in 1977 and 1999, and real estate in 1975, 1995, and 2000 were all

---

[9]While we do not have access to the more comprehensive Dimson, Marsh, Staunton data sets from *Triumph of the Optimists*, we expect the results to be confirmatory.

Blood in the Streets (*Continued*)

good times to be buying when there was blood in the streets. Now, how many of you were buying commodities in 1999, real estate in 2000, and stocks in 2003? (See Table 7.9.)

Table 7.8 Country Mean Reversion 1903–2007

	All Years	After Two Down Years in a Row	After Three Down Years in a Row
Average Return	13.02%	19.03%	30.30%
Median Return	10.65%	14.97%	19.57%
Frequency	100%	9.26%	2.59%

Table 7.9 Asset Class Mean Reversion 1975–2007

	All Years	After Two Down Years in a Row	After Three Down Years in a Row
Average Return	12.97%	23.19%	33.93%
Median Return	12.18%	28.68%	33.93%
Frequency	100%	7.27%	1.21%

The easiest way an investor can capitalize on this behavior is to rebalance, especially if an asset class has experienced a sharp drop in prices. A more involved method would be to gain additional exposure or to purchase some options (calls) on asset classes or countries that have had multiple down years in a row.

The Systems versus the Endowments

How would these two simple models for tactical asset allocation compare to the endowment returns? Let's take a look.

We have to shift back to the fiscal year end of June 30th to compare apples to apples, as well as only going back to 1985 because that is the modern era for the endowments.

Table 7.10   Timing and Rotation vs. the Endowment Returns 1985–2008, Fiscal Year Ending June 30th

	Harvard	Yale	Timing	Leveraged Timing	Rotation
Annualized Return	15.23%	16.62%	12.02%	17.95%	15.81%
Volatility	9.55%	10.40%	6.85%	13.91%	10.21%
Sharpe 5%	1.07	1.12	1.02	0.93	1.06
Best Year	32.20%	41.00%	30.50%	56.24%	47.19%
Worst Year	−2.70%	−0.20%	1.63%	−4.62%	0.72%
Correlation to Harvard	—	0.91	0.74	0.73	0.80
Correlation to Yale	0.91	—	0.72	0.70	0.79

Table 7.10 shows the returns of the timing strategy and the rotation strategy (taking the top three asset classes) versus the top endowments from 1985 to 2007, fiscal year ending June 30th. The active strategies are gross returns, so management fees, taxes, and commissions would eat into returns a bit.

The timing model does a good job of achieving a high Sharpe Ratio, but does not have near the absolute returns as the Harvard and Yale endowments. An investor can get in the vicinity of Harvard and Yale returns with the rotation model, but increased transaction costs may bring the risk-adjusted return down to the timing model's Sharpe Ratio. Overall, using a simple tactical system can possibly improve your risk-adjusted returns over a passive buy and hold allocation.

Why It Works

Because I believe that all criteria for investing (that is, good betting strategies) should have a logic that isn't time specific, I believe that the alpha generators that make up the ultimate alpha generator should be timeless and universal. By that I mean that they should have worked over very long time horizons and in all countries' markets.

RAY DALIO *2020 VISION*

We have mentioned a number of different ways to think about and quantify momentum and mean reversion in this chapter. We believe that as long as humans are involved in the financial markets, the markets will continue to be driven by the emotions of greed and fear. This aspect of the market is a simple example of an alpha generator that is "timeless and universal." Our research has shown that returns are lower and volatility is higher when asset classes are below the 10-month moving average. This increase in volatility and its clustering[10] is one of the simple reasons the timing model works – when markets are declining people become more fearful and use a different part of their brain than during periods when markets are going up.

As you can see in Table 7.11, most of the asset classes are going up about 70% of the time (as defined by being above the 10-month simple moving average). However, during the 30% or so of the time that markets are declining, they have much different characteristics than up trending markets. Returns are roughly cut by over 75%, and volatility is higher by more than 30%. A simple example of these characteristics is the volatility investors have experienced in 2008 as markets have declined. The VIX hit all-time highs in the 70s. The reasons are simple—people are uncertain, fearful, and do not know what to do. The quantitative system helps you avoid this uncertainty.

Many pundits also show how missing the ten best days of the market can decimate your returns, and use that as proof that market timing doesn't work. What they don't understand is that the vast majority (roughly 70%) of *both* the best and worst days occur when the market is below the ten-month simple moving average. The simple reason is because the market is more volatile.

Paul Gire has an informative piece in *The Journal of Financial Planning* that observes what happens when an investor misses the best days, the worst days, and both the best and worst days.

He found that from 1984 to 1998, the buy-and-hold return for this 15-year period was 17.89% per year for the Dow—one of the most bullish periods in market history. Missing the ten best days resulted in returns of 14.24% per year, while missing the worst ten days resulted in annual returns of 24.17%. However, missing both the ten worst and ten

---

[10]You could spend a lot of time studying volatility clustering, and there are fancy models called funny names like ARCH (autoregressive conditional heteroskedasticity) that attempt to describe the process.

Table 7.11   1973–2008

Asset Class	Market >10 month SMA	Market <10 Month SMA	Difference
US Stocks			
% of time	72.92%	27.08%	
Annualized Return	13.53%	3.02%	−77.67%
Annualized Volatility	13.89%	19.22%	38.38%
Foreign Stocks			
% of time	69.91%	30.09%	
Annualized Return	14.64%	1.89%	−87.08%
Annualized Volatility	14.86	21.51%	44.77%
Bonds			
% of time	76.10%	23.90%	
Annualized Return	10.08%	6.34%	−37.04%
Annualized Volatility	8.69%	10.17%	16.97%
Commodities			
% of time	66.90%	33.10%	
Annualized Return	16.21%	1.13%	−93.03%
Annualized Volatility	20.78%	19.65%	−5.43%
Real Estate			
% of time	72.45%	27.55%	
Annualized Return	14.89%	−1.44%	−109.69%
Annualized Volatility	13.51%	23.78%	75.95%
Average			
% of time	71.66%	28.34%	
Annualized Return	13.87%	2.19%	−84.22%
Annualized Volatility	14.35%	18.87%	31.49%
US Stocks 1901–2008			
% of time	69.88%	30.12%	
Annualized Return	14.42%	3.03%	−78.98%
Annualized Volatility	14.30%	24.18%	69.06%

best periods resulted in returns of 20.31%—higher than the buy and hold return (and likely with less volatility).

We have found similar results when examining when the worst and best days occur—roughly 70% of the time since 1951 they have occurred when the S&P 500 is below the 200 day SMA.

There are many, many variants and offshoots one can take from the model. For the most part, the takeaway is that for similar risk, a momentum model generates some excess annual returns. This is not the investing Holy Grail, but we consider this a method for a simple, timeless alpha that is rooted in human psychology.

> *This extraordinary achievement quite naturally attracts all the attention, yet close observers can say that the real secret to Yale's remarkable success is defense, defense, defense. But how, you might ask, can defense be so important to Yale's remarkably positive results? Starting with that great truism of long-term success in investing—if investors could just eliminate their larger losses, the good results would take care of themselves— we remind ourselves of the great advantages of staying out of trouble.*
> —CHARLES ELLIS, YALE INVESTMENT COMMITTEE CHAIRMAN

Summary

- Do not lose.
- Do not lose.
- Investing in asset classes yields rewards, but the risks can be significant.
- Most asset classes have experienced large drawdowns that can require years to recover from.
- Evolution by natural selection has resulted in numerous behavioral biases that interfere with investing success.
- Using a simple trend following approach can help to instill a disciplined investment process, while reducing volatility and risk of drawdowns.
- Historically the simple timing model has worked in virtually every market over long time frames.
- Applied to the Ivy Portfolio, the timing model results in equity-like returns with bond-like volatility, and 36 years of consecutive positive returns.

- While still trailing the endowments, the timing model approaches the risk-adjusted returns of Harvard and Yale. A leveraged version has similar returns as the endowments, albeit with stock-like volatility.
- A similar relative strength (or rotation) model could work for investors seeking higher absolute returns with manageable risk.

Chapter 8

Following the Smart Money

If I have seen further it is by standing on the shoulders of giants.
—SIR ISAAC NEWTON

Picking stocks is very difficult. Most academic research has shown that both individuals and professionals stink at it.

That being said, would anyone deny that there are some people who are very good at stock picking? Just like any other profession, there are people who are experts in their field. These top professionals get paid handsomely for what they do.

Warren Buffett certainly comes to mind. Buffett is one of the most famous stock pickers of all time, and with an estimated net worth of more than $60 billion, he is also one of the richest people in the world.

If someone told you that you could have your portfolio managed by Warren Buffett, you would be interested, right? (If you say no then quit reading this book and go visit one of those highly paid experts in the medical field.)

This chapter outlines a simple method for letting the top hedge fund managers manage your portfolio—for free. It takes no more than about 30 minutes four times a year.

After explaining how to go about tracking these managers, we will then take a look at a few examples, and see how following their picks since 2000 would have worked out. You can even go as far as taking picks from multiple managers, and form your own "hedge fund of funds." And you don't have to worry about the fund manager disappearing into the night with all your hard-earned cash.

Mebane Faber is cofounding an online software project, called AlphaClone (www.alphaclone.com) to automate the 13F processes and intelligence described in this chapter. Since we don't want this to be an advertising/promotional piece, we detail below how to complete the research on your own below.

Introduction to the 13F

There is a famous saying in poker, "If you sit down at the table and don't know who the fish is, you're the fish." Most people, when sitting down at a poker table will quickly lose all of their money to a professional player. While luck can have an influence in the short term, eventually the outcome is near certain. Most individual investors do not know they are the fish in the game known as Wall Street.

However, what if after you sat down at the table with World Series of Poker Hall of Fame member Johnny Chan, he offered to let you peek at his cards and make bets alongside of his? That would be a huge advantage. It would be silly not to look at his cards and emulate his bets. What if all of the professionals in the casino made the same offer?

Did you know you can actually look up any institutional fund's holdings online (if they have more than $100 million of assets under management), including those of the aforementioned Warren Buffett? But how many of you do that? Considering these managers often spend every waking and sleeping moment thinking and obsessing about the financial markets, are significantly more capitalized than you, and have access to far more resources than you do—wouldn't that make sense?

Following is a brief overview of the process of following these star managers, along with some case studies that back test the manager's picks to detail how the portfolios would have performed since 2000.

SEC 13Fs

In 1975 Congress passed Section 13(f) pursuant to the Securities Exchange Act of 1934. The measure required every institutional fund manager with assets under management over $100 million to report its holdings once a quarter to the Securities and Exchange Commission. Congress did this to improve the disclosure and transparency of these big firms with the hope of increasing confidence in the financial markets.

The name of the form is the "13F" (also referred to as the Form 13F-HR). The data is uploaded to the SEC web site no more than 45 days after the quarter's end, and an investor can view the holdings free

---

Goldstein versus the SEC

While Section 13(f) has been in place for over 30 years, some people are beginning to question the purpose and tangible benefits of the transparency. Philip Goldstein, the managing partner of hedge fund Bulldog Investors, filed in October 2006 a formal request for exemption from the rule. His reasoning is that the Form 13F disclosure makes public his proprietary trade secrets. Goldstein argues that the composition of his portfolio is secret intellectual property and protected under the Constitution's Fifth Amendment. While most experts believe Goldstein's request will be denied, he states publicly that he is willing to sue the SEC.

of charge, forever. By reviewing the 13Fs, you can view and understand the holdings of every manager from George Soros, to Seth Klarman, to Carl Icahn, to Warren Buffett.

Searching the SEC Database

The SEC maintains the EDGAR database (www.sec.gov/edgar. shtml),[1] and posts the electronic versions of 13F filings within a day after such filings are received. The data goes back to late 1999, although the archives in Washington, D.C., contain paper records that go back further.

All an investor has to do to retrieve the holdings is to visit the web site, and search under "Company Name" for the desired fund or company. In our first case study, we use "Berkshire Hathaway" (CIK # 0001067983) resulting in a laundry list of filings. We are interested in only the 13F filings, and the user can narrow down the list by inputting the "Form Type" provided (13F). All of the quarterly 13F filings are now at your fingertips.

Since the 13Fs are published within 45 days after quarter end, the filing for the quarter that ended December 31, 2008 would be available around February 15, 2009. Examining the most recent 13F from Berkshire reveals a list of long-time Buffett holdings including American Express, Wells Fargo, Anheuser Busch, Washington Post, and Coca-Cola.

This information is indeed interesting, but can it be of any value? Typically, the best investors to choose for this analysis are managers who employ long-term holding periods (in Buffett's case he has stated that his favorite holding period is "forever"). This will minimize the effects high turnover would have on the portfolio, and the 45-day delay in reporting times should not be a major factor in performance. (The data is 45 days "stale" when you see it, and the manager may very well not even own the stock by the time the 13F is posted.) We believe that the major value added in the investment process from these managers is in stock picking and not in investment

---

[1]Other web sites aggregate the information into more useable and searchable formats (some for a fee), including EDGAR Online, Stockpickr, and LionShares.

timing. The portfolios we will track are long-only, and focus on managers with long-term holdings. While most hedge funds short and/or use derivatives to hedge or leverage their ideas, these positions do not show up on the 13F filing.

The methodology we are going to use is as follows:

1. Download all of the 13F quarterly filings.
2. If there are more than 10 holdings, simply use the 10 largest holdings, as the majority of a manager's performance should be driven by his largest holdings.
3. Equal-weight the 10 holdings.
4. Rebalance, add/delete holdings quarterly, and calculate performance as of the 20th of the month to allow for all filings to arrive.[2]

To summarize some of the differences in managing a portfolio based on 13F filings versus allocating an investment to a hedge fund manager, the following list is helpful.

Potential benefits of the 13F strategy versus allocating to a hedge fund manager

- **Access**—Many of the best hedge funds are not open to new investment capital, and if they are many have high minimum requirements (in excess of $10 million in many cases). As Mark Yusko, owner of Morgan Creek Capital, said in *Foundations and Endowment Investing*, "We don't want to give money to people that want our money. We want to give it to people that don't want it."
- **Transparency**—The investor controls and is aware of the exact holdings at all times, thus eliminating fraud risk.
- **Liquidity**—The investor can trade out of the positions at any time, versus monthly, quarterly, or longer lockup periods at hedge funds.

---

[2]To accurately calculate returns, we included the portfolio effects of all stocks that are no longer traded due to delistings, buyouts, mergers, bankruptcies, and so on. We also include all dividends (cash, stock, special, etc.). Often, databases and backtesting software packages do not account for stocks no longer trading, which can heavily skew results. The dataset we use is provided by Alpha Clone.

- **Fees**—Most funds charge high fees, the standard is 2% management and 20% performance fees. Fund of funds layer on an additional 1% and 10%. The fees associated with managing a 13F portfolio are simply the investor's routine brokerage expenses.
- **Risk targeting**—The investor can control the hedging and leverage to suit his risk tolerances. Blow-up risk from leverage or derivatives is eliminated.
- **Tax management**—Hedge funds are typically run without regard to tax implications, while the investor can manage the positions in accordance with his tax status.

Potential drawbacks of the 13F strategy versus allocating to a hedge fund manager

- **Expertise in portfolio management**—The investor does not have access to the timing and portfolio trading capabilities of the manager (could also be a benefit).
- **Exact holdings**—Crafty hedge fund managers have some tricks to avoid revealing their holdings on 13Fs—shorting against the box and moving positions off their books at the end of the quarter are two of them. The lack of short sales and futures reporting means that the results will differ from the hedge fund results.
- **Forty-five-day delay in reporting**—The delay in reporting will affect the portfolio in various amounts for different funds due to turnover. At worst, an investor could own a position the hedge fund manager sold out of 45 days ago.
- **High turnover strategies**—Managers who employ pairs trading or strategies that trade frequently are poor candidates for 13F replication.
- **Arbitrage strategies**—13F filings may show that a manager is long a stock, when in reality he is using it in an arbitrage strategy. The short hedge will not show up on the 13F.

Let's take a look at Warren Buffett and a few of the top hedge fund managers to get a feel for how this process works.

Case Study #1: Warren Buffett

Warren Buffett is one of the most celebrated investors of all time. Buffett learned his craft from his mentor, Benjamin Graham, author of the legendary tomes *Security Analysis* and *The Intelligent Investor*. Graham ran his own investment partnership for years, grounded on the concept of buying stocks that were cheap compared to their intrinsic value. He preached about buying securities that had a "margin of safety." After a lifetime spent studying stocks, Graham stated the following in the *Financial Analysts Journal* (1976):

> In general, no. I am no longer an advocate of elaborate techniques of security analysis in order to find superior value opportunities. This was a rewarding activity, say, 40 years ago, when our textbook *Graham and Dodd* was first published; but the situation has changed a great deal since then. In the old days any well-trained security analyst could do a good professional job of selecting undervalued issues through detailed studies; but in the light of the enormous amount of research now being carried on, I doubt whether in most cases such extensive efforts will generate sufficiently superior selections to justify their cost. To that very limited extent I'm on the side of the "efficient market" school of thought now generally accepted by the professors.

And Graham came to this conclusion prior to the advent of the Internet, Bloomberg, and other modern research tools. The efficient market hypothesis (EMH) was certainly making the rounds through academia and the investing public at the time. However, Warren Buffett has famously dismissed the theory, stating, "I'd be a bum on the street with a tin cup if the markets were always efficient." Would the student be able to prove the teacher wrong?

An investor who wants exposure to Buffett's investing acumen can invest in any of the mutual funds that share the Buffett investment style. When Warren Buffett closed his investment partnership in 1969, he advised his investors to place their money in the Sequoia Fund, managed by Ruane, Cuniff & Goldfarb, Inc. (which reopened in 2008 for the first time since 1985). The Tweedy Browne family of funds is another good example—in fact, the firm was founded by several employees of the Graham-Newman partnership.

While Warren Buffett has practiced some hedge fund techniques such as trading currencies and commodities, merger arbitrage, convertible arbitrage, PIPEs, and private equity, he is known mostly for his equity investments. There have been numerous books that have tried to divine exactly how Mr. Buffett goes about selecting his investments. The American Association of Individual Investors (AAII) and web sites such as Validea.com have developed screens that are designed to find companies that Warren Buffett would buy based on criteria he has promoted in the decades of public speaking, annual reports, and prior transactions. Indeed, some investors simply buy Berkshire Hathaway stock, gaining access to his portfolio management skills, exposure to the operations of an insurance conglomerate, and entree into the Berkshire Hathaway annual shareholder meeting.

But why not just buy what Warren buys? We set out in this writing to examine whether following Berkshire Hathaway's investments utilizing Form 13Fs could offer the investor the opportunity to piggyback on Buffett's stock picks, and consequently, achieve outsized excess returns.

Following the methodology presented above, the following results for the period from 2000 to 2008 are found in Table 8.1. The "Buffett" column represents the strategy portfolio with 10 holdings equal-weighted and rebalanced quarterly, and we choose to compare those returns to the broad U.S. market (S&P 500). The first observation is how dismal the returns have been for stocks this decade. Negative returns for the entire decade with a 44% drawdown is depressing indeed.

Buffett's equity selections outperformed the indexes quite substantially. Volatility was low, surprising given that the portfolio contained only 10 holdings.

Table 8.1 Buffett 13F Clone versus the S&P 500 Total Return

2000–2008	Buffett	S&P 500
Annualized Return	6.48%	−3.50%
Volatility	13.20%	20.29%
Sharpe (3%)	0.26	−0.32
Max Drawdown	−27.80%	−44.73%
Best Year	27.8%	28.7%
Worst Year	−20.3%	−37.0%

Source: AlphaClone.

Recently, two professors examined a similar method of mimicking Buffet's portfolio through the 13F process back to 1976. They found that the portfolio outperformed the S&P 500 by over 11% per year from 1976–2006, and was higher in 27 out of 31 years!

Case Study #2: Greenlight Capital

The second fund we have chosen to track is Greenlight Capital, managed by David Einhorn. While on the subject of poker, David Einhorn won $659,730 for placing 18th in the World Series of Poker in the summer of 2006. The 37-year-old fund manager donated all of the proceeds to the Michael J. Fox Foundation for Parkinson's Research (where he also sits on the board of directors). Placing 18th out of over 8,000 entrants is an amazing accomplishment, but beating the financial markets with a 25% *net* return for the previous decade is doubly impressive.

Einhorn started his hedge fund in 1995, after being rejected from every Ph.D. economics program to which he applied. The initial $1 million starting stake has since grown to over $5 billion. Due to his strong returns, the fund has largely been closed to new investors since 2000. Investors looking for more insight into the process and stock picking methods of Einhorn can read the very good book, *Fooling Some of the People All of the Time* (2008), which details the continued battle between Einhorn and Allied Capital.

Table 8.2 looks at Greenlight's holdings since 2000 utilizing the 13F forms in an identical manner to the Buffett study. Again, it includes

Table 8.2 Greenlight 13F Clone versus the S&P 500 Total Return

2000–2008	Greenlight	S&P 500
Annualized Return	12.58%	−3.50%
Volatility	38.20%	20.29%
Sharpe (3%)	0.25	−0.32
Max Drawdown	−66.30%	−44.73%
Best Year	72.1%	28.7%
Worst Year	−48.5%	−37.0%

Source: AlphaClone.

the effects of all stocks that are no longer listed due to delistings, buy-outs, mergers, and bankruptcies.

As evidenced by Table 8.2, the 13F strategy had very strong performance with over 10% compounded annual returns. The volatility was higher than the market indices, likely due to the relatively concentrated portfolio of only 10 names, in addition to getting penalized for high upside volatility (remember Chapter 4?). Annualizing monthly figures rather than yearly would result in lower volatility numbers.

Case Study #3: Blue Ridge Capital

If you had to name the top hedge fund managers ever, Julian H. Robertson would certainly be on the list. Robertson successfully ran the Tiger Funds for many years, and an entire book is written about Robertson (*Julian Robertson: A Tiger in the Land of Bulls and Bears*). The Tiger Funds reached a peak of $22 billion in assets in 1998. After many years of strong out-performance, Robertson suffered large losses and while the Standard and Poor's 500 stock index climbed 21% in 1999, Tiger declined 19%. Tiger's largest equity holding at that time was U.S. Airways, whose troubles dragged down its overall returns. As a result of such missteps, Robertson closed his investment company in March 2000.

After shutting down portfolio management, Tiger is still in operation, albeit resembling an incubator structure for young managers. Having worked at Tiger is like possessing the hedge fund gold seal of approval. Following is a short list of "Tiger Cubs" that have since started their own funds:

- Lawrence Bowman—Bowman Capital.
- Steven Mandel—Lone Pine Capital.
- Lee Ainslie—Maverick Capital.
- John Griffin—Blue Ridge Capital.
- Andreas Halvorsen—Viking Global.
- Tom Brown—Second Curve Capital.
- Quinn Riordan—Elmwood Advisors.
- Paul Spieldenner—Bamboo Capital.
- Tom Facciola—TigerShark.
- Bill Hwang—Tiger Asia.

- Dwight Anderson—Ospraie Capital.
- Chase Coleman—Tiger Technology.
- Kevin Kenny—Emerging Sovereign.
- Patrick McCormack—Tiger Consumer.
- Paul Touradji—Touradji Capital.
- Bjorn Rise—Oceanic Energy.

John Griffin was the former right-hand man of Julian Robertson. From 1993 to 1996, he served as president of Tiger Management, which he joined in 1987 after two years as a financial analyst in the Merchant Banking Group of Morgan Stanley.

Blue Ridge Capital is an investment partnership started by Griffin in June of 1996. The firm seeks high absolute returns by owning shares in businesses with outstanding investment characteristics and selling short the stock of companies with fundamental problems. Investment decisions are based on detailed, company-specific research with a long-term time horizon—the classic valued-added research that many long-short managers strive to employ, but few master.

Griffin graduated from the University of Virginia where he now teaches the class "Advanced Seminar in Security Analysis" via a live video feed from New York (and also a similar class at Columbia University). The focus of the class is learning to conduct value-added fundamental research, and many weeks a different hedge fund manager cohosts the class.[3]

Blue Ridge follows the classic long/short mold, and derives much of its profits from its short book (which is somewhat of a hallmark of the Tiger Cubs). How would a portfolio based on the 13F submissions of Blue Ridge Capital perform? Table 8.3 reveals the answer.

The Blue Ridge portfolio shows that even though the simple 13F method can capture some of the manager's alpha, it will likely trail the returns of the underlying fund manager. For example, Griffin had a monster 2007, up over 60%. The long-only 13F strategy would have "only" done about 23%. Obviously Griffin was able to parlay shorts, derivatives,

---

[3]Mebane Faber attended the class in the spring of 2000. Fellow Virginia alumnus and Maverick Capital founder and portfolio manager Lee Ainslie was a guest speaker. Closed to new investors for more than 10 years, Maverick has consistently returned over 20% a year and has the distinction of never having had a down year since inception.

Table 8.3   Blue Ridge 13F Clone versus the S&P 500 Total Return

2000–2008	Blue Ridge	S&P 500
Annualized Return	3.25%	−3.50%
Volatility	21.78%	20.29%
Sharpe 3%	0.01	−0.32
Max Drawdown	−39.60%	−44.73%
Best Year	26.6%	28.7%
Worst Year	−33.9%	−37.0%

Source: AlphaClone.

and market timing to his advantage. He delivers quite a bit of alpha from his international positions as well as his shorts—neither of which show up on the 13F. Add on the fact that some of the positions may be short against the box, and the clone strategy will trail the manager.

When picking managers, it is best to find managers that derive the majority of their profits from their U.S. long book. But hey, 6% a year outperformance per year isn't bad!

Combining the Top Fund Managers to Create Your Own Fund of Funds

Instead of just tracking one manager, who may be going through a nasty divorce or is growing content with his wealth, an investor can create a hedge fund of funds by combining a number of funds into one portfolio. The investor could simply take the top few holdings from each fund, and update the portfolio in the same method as before. This option gives the investor the additional benefit of diversifying the risk across multiple managers. By selecting the largest, most concentrated holdings in these funds, this approach provides the additional benefit of selecting stocks in which the managers believe most strongly and have the greatest convictions.

Another application is applying a consensus approach to a portfolio. This tactic involves purchasing the stocks that are held by more than one fund manager. The thesis here is that there is verification that more than one investor has come to the same conclusion.

While we examined the results of long-only portfolios, many investors prefer less volatile portfolios. Investors could employ a simple hedging strategy, buying puts or shorting various indices to reduce volatility and market exposure. There are several variants one could explore,[4] and one of the reasons Faber is co-founding the AlphaClone software application which will support user-friendly testing of a multitude of interesting strategies.

Table 8.4 employs a fund-of-funds approach, and shows a simple portfolio of the top three positions from each of the aforementioned managers: Buffett, Einhorn, and Griffin, rebalanced quarterly.

The FOF experienced 10% a year outperformance with less than stock volatility and much less drawdown than the broad index. A more robust method would be to combine a number of managers whose methodologies differ substantially, and the volatility and drawdown should decrease further. In this case, the result was positive returns during down years for stocks in 2000, 2001, and 2002.

The individual investor has access to the brightest minds in the investment business at his fingertips, and following the best hedge funds can simplify the equity selection process. Why spend all your time

Table 8.4 13F FOF Approach

2000–2008	FOF	S&P 500
Annualized Return	7.53%	−3.50%
Volatility	17.95%	20.29%
Sharpe 3%	0.25	−0.32
Max Drawdown	−37.00%	−44.73%
Best Year	42.8%	28.7%
Worst Year	−29.4%	−37.0%

Source: AlphaClone.

---

[4]Investment banks including Goldman Sachs, Morgan Stanley, and Merrill Lynch have developed proprietary strategies that mine 13F filings. They all focus on the entire hedge fund universe, which includes results from less relevant funds for 13F replication strategies including active traders, arbitragers and the like, as well as lower-quartile performing funds.

watching CNBC and reading the *Wall Street Journal* when you can simply farm out your stock management to the most brilliant minds in the business? There are numerous funds for an investor to choose from when wading through the institutional fund jungle. Following is a list of other funds to consider:

Abingdon Capital Management
Abrams Capital
Akre Capital
Alson Capital Partners
Appaloosa Management
Atlantic Investment Management
Barrington Partners
The Baupost Group
Bridger Capital
Cannell Capital
Chesapeake Asset Management
Chieftain Capital Management
Cobalt Capital
Defiance Asset Management
Eagle Capital Partners
Eminence Capital
ESL Investments
Fine Capital Management
Glenhill Advisors
Glenview Capital Management
Gotham Capital
Highfields Capital Management
Icahn Associates
Jana Partners
King Street Capital
Lane Five Capital
Libra Advisors
Lone Pine Capital
Maverick Capital
Newcastle Partners

Omega Advisors
Pabrai Investment Funds
Pennant Capital Management
Perry Capital
Pershing Square Capital Management
Private Capital Management
Relational Investors
SAB Capital
Scion Capital
Second Curve Capital
Semper Vic Partners
Shamrock Activist Value
Steel Partners
T2 Partners
Thames River Capital
Third Point Management
Tiger Global
Tontine Capital Partners
Tracer
Trafelet Delta
ValueAct Capital Partners
Viking Global Investors
Wyser-Pratte Management
Yaupon Partners

Summary

- It is very simple to track holdings of institutional fund managers utilizing 13F filings submitted quarterly to the SEC.
- Following these fund managers can lead to new investment ideas.
- More importantly, results indicate that by tracking and rebalancing portfolios quarterly, an investor can replicate the long holdings of hedge funds without paying the high hedge fund fees.
- These excess returns can benefit from in-line volatility compared with the equity and hedge fund indices.

- Because value managers have long-term holding periods and low turnover, the 45-day delay in reported holdings should not be a significant issue.
- Case studies are presented examining three value investors, Berkshire Hathaway's Warren Buffett, Greenlight Capital's David Einhorn, and Blue Ridge Capital's John Griffin and back-tested results are presented for the portfolios since 2000.
- Additionally, more complex applications for investors could include constructing hedged portfolios, as well as portfolios that compile the holdings of multiple fund manager holdings. This "fund of funds" would add diversification to the 13F replication strategy.

Chapter 9

Develop an Action Plan

There is no more fatal blunderer than he who consumes the greater part of his life getting his living.

—HENRY DAVID THOREAU

eople often work incredibly hard at their jobs over the course of a lifetime to build an investment nest egg, and then only pay passing consideration to managing their money. Often investors do not have a framework for how they plan on investing, and many investment approaches are closer to gambling or entertainment than a well thought out plan. In many cases the investor is exposed to incredible amounts of risk without even knowing it.

If you ask people what their goal is in life, they often respond "happiness" or something similar. If people were to go about optimizing their happiness in life, many would rethink their investment program. If you believe some of the behavioral research mentioned earlier in this book, losses and downside volatility become much more of a focus than pure return. This summary chapter tries to answer one of the most often asked questions in the investment advisory business: "What do I do?"

Why not simplify your investment process? Outsourcing your strategic asset allocation to the top 1% of investors, the Super Endowments, seems like a logical first step. Implementing and monitoring the portfolio in a thoughtful and disciplined manner is a requirement for continued success. Adding active managers, using prudent risk management, and piggybacking on the top hedge funds are all possible extensions to the core portfolio to improve absolute and risk-adjusted returns.

Implementing Your Ivy Portfolio

Following is a framework for developing an investment program based on the principles outlined in *The Ivy Portfolio*.

Step 1: Select Your Policy Portfolio

The first step is to outsource your strategic asset allocation to the top 1% of institutional investors—the Super Endowments. Using the Harvard and Yale Endowment annual reports as a guide, examine their Policy Portfolios, and decide on an asset allocation that fits your personal situation. Tailoring your allocation to invest more in fixed income as you age or for more risk averse individuals is a reasonable example.

Key lessons from the Super Endowments include a focus on equity-like assets, and including diverse asset classes such as domestic stocks, foreign stocks, bonds, real estate, and commodities. The exact mix is less important than having some exposure to each of the main asset classes: stocks, bonds, and real assets. While we suggested three simple Ivy Portfolios in Chapter 4, any of the allocations in this book would suffice, depending on your risk preferences and comfort level. At the end of this chapter are repeats of some of the main portfolios we have mentioned throughout the book, and the following table depicts the simplest of the sample Ivy Portfolios.

The Ivy Portfolio	Simple
Domestic Stocks	20%
Foreign Stocks	20
Bonds	20
Real Estate	20
Commodities	20
Total	100%

Step 2: Implement Your Policy Portfolio

Avoid fees by investing in tax-efficient, low-cost index mutual funds or ETFs.

Step 3: Stick to Your Policy Portfolio with Discipline

This process lets you avoid emotional decision making and behavioral biases by sticking to a strategic asset allocation. Review your portfolio yearly. Rebalance in tax-exempt accounts yearly if positions have strayed, and with taxable accounts it makes sense to rebalance with inflows and outflows of cash. Consider using some tax harvesting strategies in taxable accounts.

Step 4: Decide If You Want Exposure to Active Managers— Hedge Funds and Private Equity

We examined the alternatives space and the available options in private equity and listed hedge funds. We recommend leaving out the private equity allocation, but if you are going to use listed private equity funds or ETF/ETNs, consider them a replacement for part of the domestic and foreign equity portfolio. Beware of the tax consequences and structure of the funds as well.

Consider listed alternative funds as additions and/or replacements to the portfolio based on their correlation to the core portfolio and their risks and strategies. For strategies that have no correlation to the core portfolio, an allocation as high as the 20% the Super Endowments utilize is not unreasonable. Again, be aware of tax issues and especially the costs of these active funds.

Step 5: Consider Active Risk Management

If you are not satisfied with an indexed portfolio of world asset classes and listed alternatives, there are some active management techniques you can use to possibly improve your absolute and risk-adjusted returns. The first is an active approach to tactical asset allocation. Sitting through long bear markets can be painful, both emotionally and financially.

An investor can use a simple trend following system to reduce the volatility and drawdowns of a portfolio. We examined how it is possible to reduce risk by selling an asset class when it declines below its long-term moving average and moving to cash. In our example we used the 10-month simple moving average. Updating this portfolio is as easy as looking up the individual asset classes once a month.[1] This tactical model would not have experienced a down year in 36 years.

Additionally, a simple rotation system based on relative strength could improve the absolute returns to a portfolio while still managing risk. This system simply selects the best performing asset classes over a specific time period. In our example, we used the average of the 3-, 6-, and 12-month total returns.

While the strategies are more tax efficient than their turnover suggests, it is preferable to run both of these active strategies in tax-deferred accounts.

Step 6: Consider Outsourcing Your Equity Portfolio to the Top Hedge Funds

Stock picking is hard. Following the top value hedge funds through 13F filings can lead to abnormal returns. Consider investing a part of the equity allocation in these managers' picks. Decide on a manager or group of managers that you want to track, and update your portfolio quarterly when the new 13F filings come out.

Step 7: Enjoy Your Life

All of the portfolios outlined are rules-based and free of emotional biases that can cloud your decision making. Isn't that the point at the end of the day? The investment portfolio is a means to an end, not an end in itself.

> *And joy is, after all, the end of life. We do not live to eat and make money. We eat and make money to be able to live. That is what life means and what life is for.*
>
> —George Mallory

---

[1] Stockcharts.com is a good service. We will update the timing model on the book web site as well, www.theivyportfolio.com.

Portfolios Discussed in *The Ivy Portfolio*

The following are a few of the sample portfolios we have mentioned throughout the book. Table 9.1 is the simplest of the portfolios with five asset classes. Table 9.2 and 9.3 further break out the asset classes into 10 and 20 holdings.

The next tables show the approximate allocations for Harvard and Yale, both without alternatives (Table 9.4) and with alternatives (Table 9.5).

Table 9.1   Simple Ivy Portfolio, 5 Asset Classes

	Ivy Portfolio	ETF
Domestic Stocks	20%	VTI
Foreign Stocks	20	VEU
Bonds	20	BND
Real Estate	20	VNQ
Commodities	20	DBC
Total	**100%**	—

Table 9.2   Simple Ivy Portfolio, 10 Asset Classes

	Ivy Portfolio	ETFs
Domestic Large Cap	10%	VTI
Domestic Small Cap	10	VB
Foreign Developed Stocks	10	VEU
Foreign Emerging Stocks	10	VWO
Domestic Bonds	10	BND
TIPS	10	TIP
Real Estate	10	VNQ
Foreign Real Estate	10	RWX
Commodities	10	DBC
Commodities	10	GSG
Total	**100%**	—

Table 9.3   Simple Ivy Portfolio, 20 Asset Classes

	Ivy Portfolio	ETFs
Domestic Large Cap	5%	VTI
Domestic Mid Cap	5	VO
Domestic Small Cap	5	VB
Domestic Micro Cap	5	IWC
Foreign Developed Stocks	5	VEU
Foreign Emerging Stocks	5	VWO
Foreign Developed Small Cap	5	GWX
Foreign Emerging Small Cap	5	EWX
Domestic Bonds	5	BND
TIPS	5	TIP
Foreign Bonds	5	BWX
Emerging Bonds	5	ESD
Real Estate	5	VNQ
Foreign Real Estate	5	RWX
Infrastructure	5	IGF
Timber	5	TREE.L
Commodities	5	DBA
Commodities	5	DBE
Commodities	5	DBB
Commodities	5	DBP
Total	**100%**	—

Table 9.4   Harvard and Yale without Alternatives (Rounded)

	Harvard 2007	Yale 2007	ETFs
Domestic Stocks	15.00%	20.00%	VTI
Foreign Developed Stocks	15.00	10.00	VEU
Foreign Emerging Stocks	15.00	15.00	VWO
Bonds	10.00	5.00	BND
TIPS	10.00	0.00	TIP
Real Estate	10.00	25.00	VNQ
Commodities	25.00	25.00	DBC
Total	**100%**	**100%**	

Table 9.5 Harvard and Yale with Alternatives (Rounded)

	Harvard 2007	Yale 2007	ETFs
Domestic Stocks	10.00%	10.00%	VTI
Foreign Developed Stocks	10.00	5.00	VEU
Foreign Emerging Stocks	10.00	10.00	VWO
Bonds	10.00	5.00	BND
TIPS	5.00	—	TIP
Real Estate	10.00	15.00	VNQ
Commodities	15.00	15.00	DBC
Private Equity	10.00	20.00	PSP/PFP
Hedge Funds	20.00	20.00	*
Total	**100%**	**100%**	

*Hedge funds can be invested in utilizing either the U.S. or foreign listed funds. Funds with high correlations to existing asset classes should be used as substitutions for existing allocations.

Appendix A

A Brief Review of Momentum and Trend Following

Strategies that rely on momentum work because the market exhibits momentum (positive serial correlation) due to underreaction and overreaction at different time frames. Momentum strategies have been in existence for the majority of the twentieth century (and probably longer). Efficient market theorists have long been puzzled by momentum and exclaim that it should not be possible to make money from buying past winners and selling past losers in well-functioning markets. Practitioners have been ignoring these efficient market theorists and collecting money for decades.

Alfred Cowles and Herbert Jones found evidence of momentum as early as the 1930s (1937). H.M. Gartley (1945) mentions methods of relative strength stock selection in his *Financial Analysts Journal* article "Relative Velocity Statistics: Their Application in Portfolio Analysis." Robert Levy (1968) identified his own system in "The Relative Strength Concept of Common Stock Price Forecasting." Other literature penned by investors who suggest using momentum in stock selection include James O'Shaughnessy's (1998) book, *What Works on Wall Street*, Martin Zweig's (1986) *Winning on Wall Street*, William O'Neil's (1988) *How to Make Money in Stocks*, and Nicolas Darvas's (1960) *How I Made $2,000,000 in the Stock Market*.

A great review of the momentum literature is included in the appendix of *Smarter Investing in Any Economy* by Mike Carr.

One of the most comprehensive studies was performed by Elroy Dimson, Paul Marsh, and Mike Staunton of *Triumph of the Optimists* fame. They found that winners (top 20% past returns) beat losers (bottom 20%) by 10.8% per year in the U.K. equity market from 1956–2007. Even using the top 100 U.K. stocks by market cap still produced a 7% outperformance. Taking a look at these top 100 stocks since 1900, they found a 10.3% per year outperformance.

Cole Wilcox and Eric Crittenden (2005) in *Does Trend Following Work on Stocks?* take up the question applied to the domestic equities market, and conclude that trend following can work well on individual equities even when adjusting for corporate actions, survivorship bias, liquidity, and transaction costs.

The momentum effect has been found in most major developed markets around the world. Narasimhan Jegadeesh and Sheridan Titman (1993) show that stocks that perform well (poorly) over a 3- to 12-month period continue to perform well (poorly) over the subsequent 3 to 12 months. The authors illustrated in 2001 that momentum strategies performed well in the subsequent out-of-sample period of the 1990s. K. Geert Rouwenhorst (1998) reports that momentum strategies are profitable in the European market as well. A good overview of the behavioral biases that may lead to the momentum effect can be found in the working paper "Momentum" by Jegadeesh and Titman (2001).

While most studies focus on individual securities, there have been some that show evidence of momentum in asset class returns as well. Kalok Chan, Allaudeen Hameed, and Wilson Tong (2000) illustrate that international stock market indexes exhibit momentum.

Two of the oldest and most discussed trend following systems are the Dow Theory, developed by Charles Dow, and the Four Percent Model developed by Ned Davis. *The Research Driven Investor* by Timothy Hayes (2001), and *Winning on Wall Street* by Martin Zweig (1986), present good reviews of each system, respectively.

The group at Merriman Capital Management (MCM)[1] has completed a number of quantitative back tests utilizing market timing on

---

[1]The web site FundAdvice.com has more information.

various asset classes, namely equities, bonds, and gold. The group uses its own strategies to manage client money, and the results presented in this book both verify and extend the work they have completed over the years. Dennis Tilley and Paul Merriman (1999–2002) describe the characteristics of a market timing system as well as the emotional and behavioral difficulties in following such a system.

An entirely different product area where trend following is heavily utilized is in the futures arena. Many global macro hedge funds and commodity-trading advisors (CTAs), such as John Henry and Bill Dunn, have been using trend following systems on futures for years, amassing billions of dollars under management. While futures trend following is quite a different strategy than what is detailed in this book, John Mulvey, Koray Simsek, and Shiv Siddhant Kaul (2005) present a description of the components of the total return of a futures trend following strategy. The return consists of collateral yield (cash sitting in T-bills), trend following gains, and rebalancing gains in order of return contribution. They assert that collateral yield is the largest chunk of return, a point often overlooked. You can get more information on CTA funds on IASG.com, as well as white papers from Standard & Poor's on the Diversified Trend Indicator.

Appendix B

Additional Charts

Following are additional charts for reference and further study. (See Figures B.1 through B.14.) They were not included in the text in order to simplify the material.

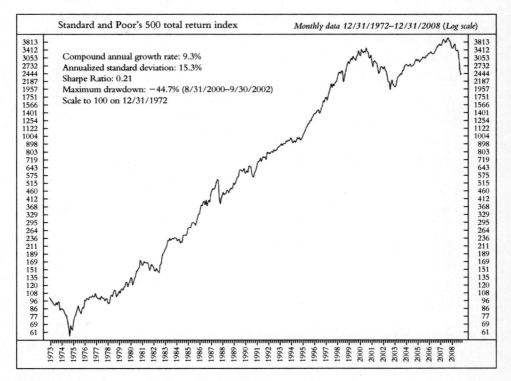

Figure B.1   S&P 500 Total Return 1973–2008
© Copyright 2008 Ned Davis Research, Inc.

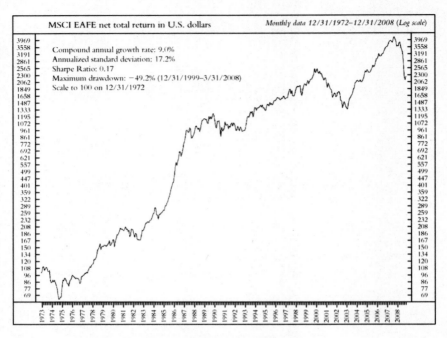

Figure B.2   MSCI EAFE Net Total Return 1973–2008
© Copyright 2008 Ned Davis Research, Inc.

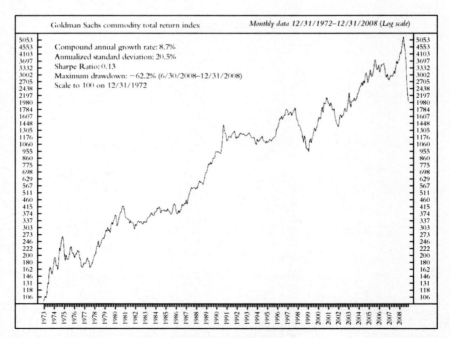

Figure B.3   GSCI Total Return Index 1973–2008
© Copyright 2008 Ned Davis Research, Inc.

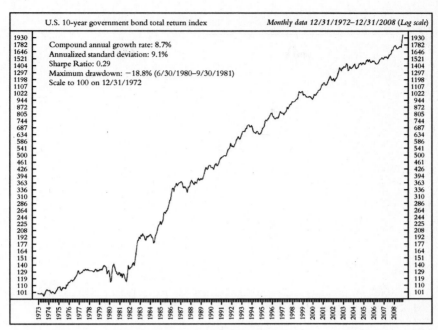

Figure B.4 10-Year U.S. Government Bond Total Return 1973–2008
© Copyright 2008 Ned Davis Research, Inc.

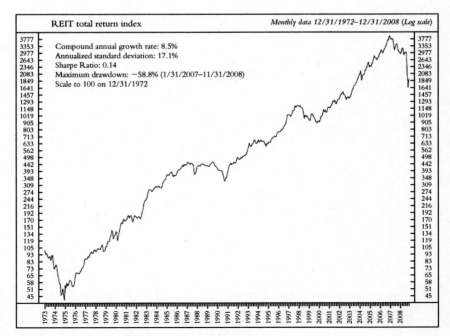

Figure B.5 REIT Total Return 1973–2008
© Copyright 2008 Ned Davis Research, Inc.

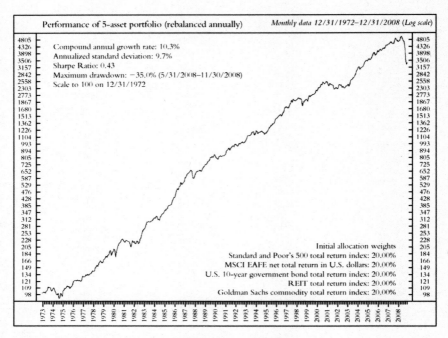

Figure B.6 Ivy Portfolio Rebalanced Annually 1973–2008
© Copyright 2008 Ned Davis Research, Inc.

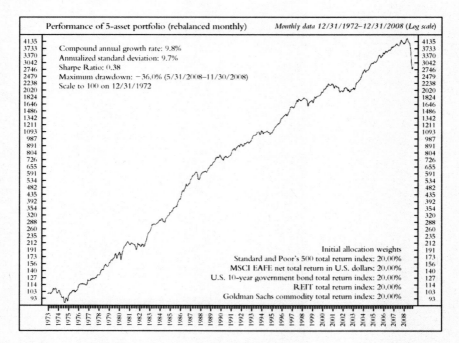

Figure B.7 Ivy Portfolio Rebalanced Monthly
© Copyright 2008 Ned Davis Research, Inc.

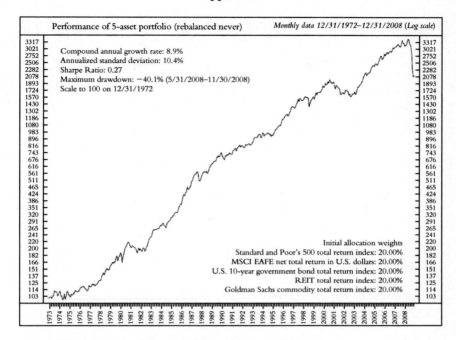

Figure B.8   Ivy Portfolio Rebalanced Never 1973–2008
© Copyright 2008 Ned Davis Research, Inc.

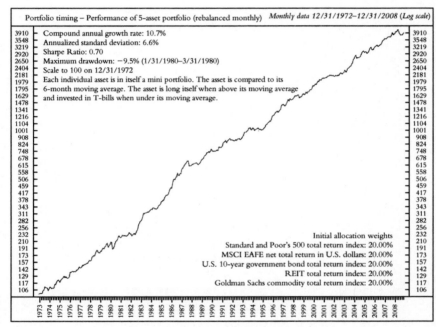

Figure B.9   6-Month Moving Average Timing Model on the Ivy
Portfolio Rebalanced Monthly
© Copyright 2008 Ned Davis Research, Inc.

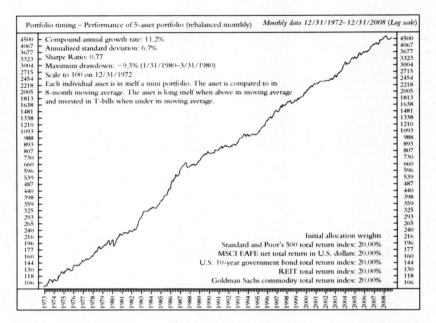

Figure B.10   8-Month Moving Average Timing Model on the Ivy Portfolio
Rebalanced Monthly
© Copyright 2008 Ned Davis Research, Inc.

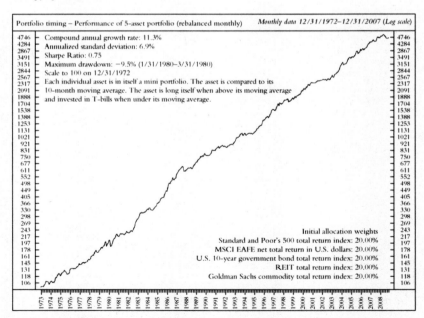

Figure B.11   10-Month Moving Average Timing Model on the
Ivy Portfolio Rebalanced Monthly
© Copyright 2008 Ned Davis Research, Inc.

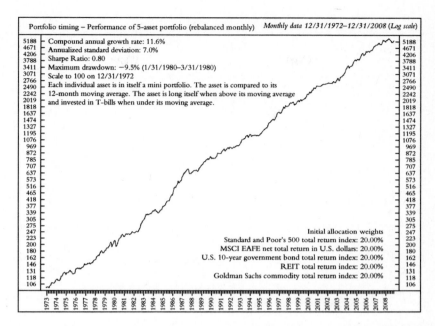

Figure B.12 12-Month Moving Average Timing Model on the Ivy Portfolio Rebalanced Monthly

© Copyright 2008 Ned Davis Research, Inc.

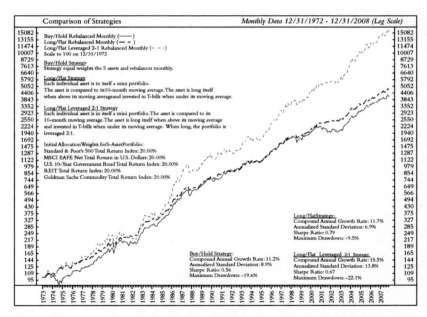

Figure B.13 The Ivy Portfolio vs. the Timing Model and the Leveraged Timing Model

© Copyright 2008 Ned Davis Research, Inc.

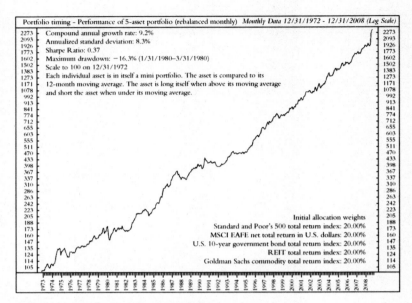

Figure B.14   The Long/Short Timing Model
© Copyright 2008 Ned Davis Research, Inc.

Appendix C

Recommended Reading

I have said that in my whole life, I've known no wise person over a broad subject matter area who didn't read all the time—none, zero. Now I know all kinds of shrewd people who by staying within a narrow area can do very well without reading. But investment is a broad area. So if you think you're going to be good at it and not read all the time, you have a different idea than I do. . . . You'd be amazed at how much Warren [Buffett] reads. You'd be amazed at how much I read.
—CHARLIE MUNGER IN *POOR CHARLIE'S ALMANACK*, 2ND EDITION, PAGE 6

While this book is meant for the general public, it would help to have a little background knowledge on some of the topics. Some recommendations follow (we especially recommend *Asset Allocation* by Roger Gibson). For full publication information, see the Bibliography.

Asset Allocation

Asset Allocation by Roger Gibson
All About Asset Allocation by Richard Ferri
The Intelligent Asset Allocator by William Bernstein
Mastering the Art of Asset Allocation by David Darst

Endowment Investing

Unconventional Success and *Pioneering Portfolio Management* by David Swensen

When Markets Collide by Mohamed El-Erian

Foundation and Endowment Investing by Lawrence Kochard and Cathleen M. Rittereiser

Trustee Investment Strategy for Endowments and Foundations by Chris Russell

History of Markets

Triumph of the Optimists: 101 Years of Global Investment Returns by Elroy Dimson, Paul Marsh, and Mike Staunton

Stocks for the Long Run by Jeremy Siegel

The Misbehavior of Markets by Benoit Mandelbrot

Manias, Panics, and Crashes by Charles Kindleberger

Extraordinary Popular Delusions and the Madness of Crowds by Charles Mackay

Reminiscences of a Stock Operator by Edwin LeFèvre

When Genius Failed by Roger Lowenstein

Capital Ideas Evolving and *Against the Gods* by Peter Bernstein

Fooled by Randomness by Nassim Nicholas Taleb

Ibbotson Yearbook by Ibbotson Associates

The CRB Commodity Yearbook by Commodity Research Bureau

The Essays of Warren Buffett by Warren E. Buffett and Lawrence A. Cunningham

Fortune's Formula by William Poundstone

Behavioral Psychology and Evolutionary Biology

Dr. Tatiana's Sex Advice to All Creation by Olivia Judson

Your Money and Your Brain by Jason Zweig

Behavioral Investing: A Practitioners Guide to Applying Behavioral Finance by James Montier

Hedge Funds

All About Hedge Funds by Robert Jaeger
Absolute Returns by Alexander Ineichen
Handbook of Alternative Investments by Mark Anson
Rocking Wall Street by Gary Marks

Profiles of Fund Managers

Hedge Hunters by Katherine Burton
2020 Vision by Harry Liem
The New Investment Superstars by Lois Peltz
Market Wizards and *The New Market Wizards* by Jack Schwager
Inside the House of Money by Stephen Drobny

Quantitative and Technical Analysis

The Research Driven Investor by Tim Hayes
Being Right or Making Money by Ned Davis
The Little Book That Beats the Market by Joel Greenblatt
The Handbook of Portfolio Mathematics by Ralph Vince
Quantitative Investment Analysis by Richard DeFusco, Dennis McLeavey, Jerald Pinto, and David Runkle

Private Equity

Private Equity as an Asset Class by Guy Fraser-Sampson
J-Curve Exposure by Pierre-Yves Mathonet and Thomas Meyer

Bibliography

Advisor Perspectives, interview with William F. Sharpe (October 16, 2007), www. advisorperspectives.com.

Appell, Douglas. "Making the Grade: Face to Face with Harvard's Mohamed El-Erian." *Pensions and Investments* (September 3, 2007).

Chen, Hsiu-Lang, N. Jegadeesh, and R. Wermers. "The Value of Active Mutual Fund Management: An Examination of the Stockholdings and Trades of Fund Managers." *Journal of Financial and Quantitative Analysis 35* (3) (2000): 343–368.

Arnold, Chris. "Yale's Money Guru Shares Wisdom with Masses." National Public Radio (October 2006).

Barber, Brad M., and Terrance Odean. "Trading Is Hazardous to Your Wealth: The Common Stock Investment Performance of Individual Investors." *Journal of Finance 45* (2) (2000): 773–806.

Benjamin, Jeff. "Hedge Funds Grew 14.5% in 2007." *Investment News* (April 7, 2008).

Bernstein, Peter L. *Capital Ideas Evolving.* New York: John Wiley & Sons, 2007.

Biggs, Barton. *Hedgehogging.* New York: John Wiley & Sons, 2006.

Bogle, John C. *The Little Book of Common Sense Investing: The Only Way to Guarantee Your Fair Share of Stock Market Returns.* New York: John Wiley & Sons, 2007.

Bogle, John C. "The Money Game." *Fortune* (October 2005).

The Boston Consulting Group. "The Advantage of Persistence: How the Best Private-Equity Firms 'Beat the Fade,' " Boston, February 2008.

Bridgewater Daily Observations, Hedge Funds Levering Betas, Bridgewater, Data, URL.

Brinson, Gary P., L. Randolph Hood, and Gilbert L. Beebower. "Determinants of Portfolio Performance." *Financial Analysts Journal*, *42* (4) (1986): 39–48 (reprinted in the *Financial Analysts Journal* 51(1) (1995): 133–138, 50th anniversary issue).

Brinson, Gary P., Brian D. Singer, and Gilbert L. Beebower. "Determinants of Portfolio Performance II: An Update," *Financial Analysts Journal* 47(3) (1991): 40–48.

Brown, Keith C., Lorenzo Garlappi, and Cristian Ioan Tiu. "The Troves of Academe: Asset Allocation, Risk Budgeting, and the Investment Performance of University Endowment Funds," McCombs Research Paper Series No. FIN-03-07, August 8, 2007.

Buffett, Warren. Berkshire Hathaway 2005 Annual Report, Chairman's Letter.

Burton, Katherine. *Hedge Hunters: Hedge Fund Masters on the Rewards, the Risk, and the Reckoning*. New York: Bloomberg Press, 2007.

Carhart, Mark. "On Persistence in Mutual Fund Performance." *Journal of Finance*, *52* (1) (1997): 57–81.

Coaker, William J. "Emphasizing Low-Correlated Assets: The Volatility of Correlation," *The Journal of Financial Planning*, September 2007.

Coaker, William J. "The Volatility of Correlation." *The Journal of Financial Planning*, September 2007.

Chan, K., A. Hameed, and W. Tong. "Profitability of Momentum Strategies in International Equity Markets." *Journal of Financial and Quantitative Analysis*, *35*, (2000): 153–172.

Carlson, Chuck. "Bountiful Harvest," *Wealth Manager Magazine*, December 1, 2007.

Covel, M.W. "Trend Following: How Great Traders Make Millions in Up or Down Markets." *Financial Times,* Prentice-Hall, 2005.

Cowles, Alfred, and Herbert E. Jones. "Some A Posteriori Probabilities in Stock Market Action." *Econometrica* Volume *5*, Issue 3 (July 1937): 280–294.

Dalbar, Inc. Quantitative Analysis of Investor Behavior, 2008.

Darst, David M. *Mastering the Art of Asset Allocation*. New York: McGraw-Hill, 2007.

Daniel, Kent, Mark Grinblatt, Sheridan Titman, and Russ Wermers. "Measuring Mutual Fund Performance with Characteristic-Based Benchmarks." *Journal of Finance 52* (3) (1997): 1035–1058. Also in Papers and Proceedings, Fifty-Seventh Annual Meeting, American Finance Association, New Orleans, January 4–6, 1997 (published July 1997).

Davidson, James, and William Rees-Mogg. *Blood in the Streets: Investment Profits in a World Gone Mad*. New York: Summit Books, 1987.

DeBondt, Werner F.M., and Richard H. Thaler. "Does the Stock Market Overreact?" *Journal of Finance* (40) (1985) 557–581.

Dichev, Ilia D. "What are Stock Investors' Actual Historical Returns? Evidence from Dollar-Weighted Returns," *American Economic Review*, 2007, vol. 97, issue 1: 386–401.

Einhorn, David. *Fooling Some of the People All of the Time: A Long Short Story*. New York: John Wiley & Sons, 2008.

El-Erian, Mohamed. *When Markets Collide: Investment Strategies for the Age of Global Economic Change*, New York: McGraw-Hill, 2008.

Faber, Mebane. "A Quantitative Approach to Tactical Asset Allocation." *The Journal of Wealth Management*. (Spring 2007).

Fisher, Philip. *Common Stocks and Uncommon Profits*. New York: Harper & Brothers, 1960.

Fraser-Sampson, Guy. *Private Equity as an Asset Class*. Sussex: John Wiley & Sons. 2007.

Fung, William, and David Hsieh. "Hedge Funds: An Industry in Its Adolescence," Federal Reserve Bank of Atlanta, Economic Review, Fourth Quarter, 2006.

Gannon, N., and M. Blum. "After Tax Returns on Stocks Versus Bonds for the High Tax Bracket Investor." *The Journal of Wealth Management* (Fall 2006).

Gartley, H.M. 1945. "Relative Velocity Statistics: Their Application in Portfolio Analysis." *Financial Analysts Journal* (April 1945): 60–64.

Gibson, Roger. *Asset Allocation* 4th Edition. New York: McGraw-Hill, 2007.

Gire, Paul. "Missing the Ten Best," *The Journal of Financial Planning* (May 2005).

Graham, Benjamin. "A Conversation with Benjamin Graham." *Financial Analysts Journal. 32* (5) September/October1976: 20–23.

Griffin, John M., and Jin Xu. "How Smart Are the Smart Guys? A Unique View from Hedge Fund Stock Holdings." Working Paper, University of Texas.

Hagstrom, Robert. *The Warren Buffett Way*. New York: John Wiley & Sons, 2005.

Harvard University Management Company, 2001–2008. Harvard University Financial Report—2000–2007, Cambridge: Harvard University.

Hayes, T. *The Research Driven Investor*. New York: McGraw-Hill, 2001.

Henriksson, Roy D., and Robert C. Merton. "On Market Timing and Investment Performance. II. Statistical Procedures for Evaluating Forecasting Skills." *Journal of Business*, University of Chicago Press, *54* (4) (October 1981) 513–533.

Hsu, David H. "What Do Entrepreneurs Pay for Venture Capital Affiliation?" (November 11, 2002). University of Pennsylvania: Wharton School Working Paper.

Ibbotson, Roger G., and Paul D. Kaplan. "Does Asset Allocation Policy Explain 40, 90, or 100 Percent of Performance?" *Financial Analysts Journal. 56* (1) (2000) 26–33.

Ibbotson, Roger G., and Peng Chen. "The A,B,Cs of Hedge Funds: Alphas, Betas, and Costs" (September 2006).Yale ICF Working Paper No. 06–10.

Idzorek, Thomas. "Private Equity and Strategic Asset Allocation." Red Rocks Capital and Ibbotson Associates, 2006.

Idzorek, Thomas. "Strategic Asset Allocation and Commodities." PIMCO and Ibbotson Associates, 2006.

Jegadeesh, Narasimhan, and Sheridan Titman. "Returns to Buying Winners and Selling Losers: Implications for Stock Market Efficiency." *Journal of Finance* (48) (1993): 65–91.

Jegadeesh, Narasimhan, and Sheridan Titman. 2001, "Momentum." University of Illinois Working Paper.

Johnson, Carla. "Greenwich Van Leads Investable Hedge Fund Indices." InvestorsOffshore.com.

Kahneman, Daniel, and Amos Tversky. "Prospect Theory: An Analysis of Decision under Risk." *Econometrica* 47(2) 1979.

Kaplan, Steven N., and Antoinette Schoar. "Private Equity Performance: Returns, Persistence and Capital Flows." (November 2003). MIT Sloan Working Paper No. 4446–03; AFA 2004 San Diego Meetings.

Kindleberger, Charles P. *Manias, Panics, and Crashes: A History of Financial Crises*, London: Pan Macmillan, 1981.

King, Matthew, and Binbin Guo. "Passive Momentum Asset Allocation." *The Journal of Wealth Management* (Winter 2002).

Knowlton, Christopher. "How the Richest Colleges Handle Their Billions." *Fortune* October 1987.

Kochard, Lawrence E., and Cathleen M. Rittereiser. *Foundation and Endowment Investing: Philosophies and Strategies of Top Investors and Institutions*, New York: John Wiley & Sons, 2008.

Kosowski, Robert, Allan Timmerman, Hal White, and Russ Wermers. "Can Mutual Fund 'Stars' Really Pick Stocks? New Evidence from a Bootstrap Analysis," Working Paper, 2001.

LeFèvre, Edwin. *Reminiscences of a Stock Operator*. New York: Doran and Co., 1923.

Lerner, Josh, Antoinette Schoar, and Jialan Wang. "Secrets of the Academy: The Drivers of University Endowment Success" (October 2007). Harvard Business School Finance Working Paper No. 07–066.

Lerner, Josh, Antoinette Schoar, and Wan Wang. "Smart Institutions, Foolish Choices? The Limited Partner Performance Puzzle." (January 2005) MIT Sloan Research Paper No. 4523–05.

Lerner, Josh, Antoinette Schoar, and Wan Wongsunwai. (2007) "Smart institutions, foolish choices: The limited partner performance puzzle. *The Journal of Finance*, 62 (2):731–764.

Lerner, Josh. "Yale University Investments Office: August 2006." Harvard Business School Publishing.

Levy, Robert. "The Relative Strength Concept of Common Stock Price Forcasting." *Investors Intelligence* (1968).

Liang, Bing. "Hedge Funds: The Living and the Dead." *Journal of Financial and Quantitative Analysis 35* (3) (September 2001): 309–326.

Liem, Harry. *2020 Vision: Investment Wisdom for Tomorrow*. Melbourne, Australia: Michael Hanrahan Publishing Services, 2007.

Lowenstein, Roger. *When Genius Failed: The Rise and Fall of Long-Term Capital Management*. New York: Random House, 2001.

Mackay, Charles. *Extraordinary Popular Delusions and the Madness of Crowds*. Boston: L.C. Page and Co., 1932.

Malkiel, Burton G., and Atanu Saha. "Hedge Funds: Risk and Return." *Financial Analysts Journal 61* (6) (2005).

Markowitz, Harry. "Portfolio Selection." *The Journal of Finance 7* (1) (March 1952): 77–91.

Martellini, Lionel, and Felix Goltz, *Hedge Fund Indices for Style Allocation*, Edhed Hedge Fund Days 2006.

Martin Gerald S., and John Puthenpurackal, *Imitation is the Sincerest Form of Flattery:* Warren Buffett and Berkshire Hathway (April 15, 2008). Available at: http://papers.ssrn.com/sol3/papers.cfm?abstract_id=806246.

Mauldin, J. Ed. *Just One Thing*. New York: John Wiley & Sons, 2005.

McVey, Henry. "Watching the Smart Money." *U.S. Portfolio Strategy*, Morgan Stanley 2006.

Merriman, Paul. "The Best Retirement Portfolio We Know," www.fundadvice.com, 2006.

Merriman, Paul. "All About Market Timing," www.fundadvice.com, 2001.

Merriman, Paul. "The Best Retirement Strategy I Know Using Active Risk Management," www.fundadvice.com, 2002.

Merriman, Paul. "Market Timing's Bad Rap," www.fundadvice.com, 2002.

Mulvey, John, Shiv Siddhant Kaul, and Koray Simsek. "Evaluating a Trend-Following Commodity Index for Multi-Period Asset Allocation." EDHEC Risk and Asset Management Research Centre, 2005.

Phalippou, Ludovic, and Oliver Gottschalg. "Performance of Private Equity Funds." EFA 2005 Moscow Meetings.

Pojarliev, Momtchil T., and Richard M. Levich. "Do Professional Currency Managers Beat the Benchmark?" NBER Working Paper No. 13714 (December 2007).

Ribeiro, Ruy, and Jan Loeys. "Exploiting Cross-Market Momentum," *J.P. Morgan Investment Strategies No. 14, 2006*.

Rouwenhoust, K. Geert. "International Momentum Strategies," *Journal of Finance* (53) (1998): 267–284.

Shea, Christopher. "U. of Rochester to Cut Programs, Faculty, and Enrollment." *The Chronicle of Higher Education, 42* (16), A33 1995.

Siegel, Jeremy J. *Stocks for the Long Run.* New York: McGraw-Hill, 2002: 283–297.

Sperandeo, Victor. *Trader Vic on Commodities,* New York: John Wiley & Sons, 2008.

Stein, Charles. "Harvard's $12 billion man." *The Boston Globe* (October 17, 2004).

Stewart, James. "A League of Their Own." *Smart Money* (September 2007).

Swensen, David. *Pioneering Portfolio Management: An Unconventional Approach to Institutional Investment.* New York: Free Press, 2000.

Swensen, David. *Unconventional Success: A Fundamental Approach to Personal Investment.* New York: Free Press, 2005.

Symonds, William. "How to Invest Like Harvard." *BusinessWeek* (December 27, 2004).

Taylor, Brain. GFD Guide to Total Returns on Stocks, Bonds and Bills. Global Financial Data, Inc., *http://www.globalfinancialdata.com/*

Thaler, Richard. *Nudge: Improving Decisions About Health, Wealth, and Happiness.* Yale University Press, 2008.

Thorp, Edward. *Beat the Dealer: A Winning Strategy for the Game of Twenty-One.* New York: Vintage, 1966.

Tilley, Dennis. "Which Is Better, Buy-and-Hold or Market Timing?" www.fundadvice.com, 1999.

Tilley, Dennis. "Designing a Market Timing System to Maximize the Probability It Will Work." www.fundadvice.com, 1999.

Tilson, Whitney. "Applying Behavioral Finance to Value Investing the Warren Buffett Way." November 2005, www.tilsonfunds.com/TilsonBehavioralFinance.pdf.

The Vanguard Group. Sources of Portfolio Performance: The Enduring Importance of Asset Allocation (Valley Forge, Pa.: Investment Counseling & Research, The Vanguard Group).

The Vanguard Group, 2006, "Understanding Alternative Investments: A primer on Hedge Fund Evaluation" (Valley Forge, Pa.: Investment Counseling & Research, The Vanguard Group).

Train, John. *The Money Masters.* New York: Harper Business, 1994.

Van, George, and Zhiyi Song. "Malkiel-Saha Hedge Fund Paper Flawed." Working paper, December 2004.

Vickers, Marcia. "Global Guru." *Fortune* (May 31, 2007).

Vigeland, Carl A. *Great Good Fortune: How Harvard Makes Its Money.* Boston: Houghton Mifflin, 1986.

Wilcox, Cole, and Eric Crittenden. "Does Trend Following Work on Stocks?" *The Technical Analyst, 14* (2005).

Yale University Investment Office, 2001–2008, The Yale Endowment—2000–2007, New Haven: Yale University.

Zachary, Seward. "Harvard's Billion-Dollar Man Departs." *Fortune,* June 29, 2005.

Zheng, Lu. "Is Money Smart? A Study of Mutual Fund Investors' Fund Selection Ability." *Journal of Finance 54* (3): 901, 1999.

Ziemba, Rachel E. S., and William T. Ziemba. *Scenarios for Risk Management and Global Investment Strategies.* New York: John Wiley & Sons, 2008.

Zweig, Jason. *Your Money and Your Brain: How the New Science of Neuroeconomics Can Help Make You Rich.* New York: Simon & Schuster, 2007.

Zweig, Martin. *Winning on Wall Street.* New York: Warner Books, Inc., 1986.

About the Authors

Mebane T. Faber, CAIA, CMT researches and manages a number of quantitative strategies at Cambria Investment Management, Inc. including equity and global tactical asset allocation portfolios. Faber is a frequent speaker and writer on quantitative asset allocation strategies. Prior to joining Cambria, Faber's background included positions as a biotechnology equity analyst and as a quantitative research analyst. Faber graduated from the University of Virginia with a double major in Engineering Science and Biology.

Eric W. Richardson is the president of Cambria Investment Management, Inc. Richardson also serves as president of the general partner of Cambria Investment Fund, LP, a fund that makes bridge loans and structured equity investments in private and publicly traded emerging growth companies. Prior to forming Cambria Investment Management and the Cambria Investment Fund, Richardson served as president and portfolio manager of Kwai Financial. Richardson began his career as a corporate and banking attorney with Milbank, Tweed, Hadley & McCloy. Richardson received his B.A. in 1988 from the University of Southern California and his J.D. in 1991 from the University of Michigan Law School.

For more information about The Ivy Portfolio and the authors, visit their web sites:

www.theivyportfolio.com
www.cambriainvestments.com
www.mebanefaber.com

Or e-mail the authors at ivy@cambriainvestments.com.

Index

Absolute return, 39, 97
Access, 175
Ackman, William, 121
AHL Core, 121
Allied Capital, 95
Alpha, 31, 140, 166
AlphaClone, 172, 183
Alternative beta, 117
Alternative Investment
    Strategies Ltd., 122, 127
Altin AG, 122
American Association of
    Individual Investors
    (AAII), 178
Anchoring, 139–140
Andreassen, Paul, 139
Arbitrage, 45–46, 118
Asness, Clifford, 31
Asset classes:

allocation within Harvard
    endowment, 50–53, 191–193
allocation within Yale
    endowment, 191–193
annual returns of Harvard and
    Yale endowments, 58
and beta, 30
Harvard endowment
    performance, 52
performance, 29, 137
and risk, 30
Yale endowment performance,
    33
Assets, illiquid, 5, 37

Bear market, 146
Beating the Dow (O'Higgins), 119
Behavioral finance, 138
Benchmark indexes, 30, 32, 85–92

Berkowitz, Bruce, 118
Berkshire Hathaway, 65, 166, 174, 177–179
Beta, 30–31, 117
Bias, 86, 95, 107, 138–140, 188
Blackstar Funds, 72
Black Swan, The (Taleb), 72, 148
Blood in the Streets: Investment Profits in a World Gone Mad (Davidson), 163
Blue Ridge Capital, 180–182
Bogle, Jack, 71
Bok, Derek, 43
Bonds, 28–29, 62
Bonds, U.S. government, 26–27, 153, 201
Boston University, 7
Boussard & Gavaudan Holding Ltd., 125–126
Buffett, Warren, 106, 135, 139–140, 171, 176–179
Building-blocks method, 70
Bulldog Investors, 173
Buy-and-hold Policy Portfolio, 77
Buybacks, 120
Buyout, 38, 84, 90

Cabot, Paul, 43–44
Cabot, Walter, 44
Calmar ratio, 66
Cambium Global Timberland (TREE.L), 48
Cambridge Associates, 85–86, 87
Capital asset pricing model (CAPM), 70
Capital gains, 161
Carr, Mike, 74

Carried interest, 86
Carry, 115
CGM Focus Fund, 118
Chan, Johnny, 173
Claymore/Clear Global Timber (CUT) exchange traded fund, 47
Closed-end funds, 36, 115
Clustering, 167
Commodities, 69–70, 116
Common Stocks and Uncommon Profits (Fisher), 139
Compounding, 146
Convexity Capital Management, 49
Correlations, 25–27
Covel, Michael, 141
Covered calls, 118
CPI-U, 11
CreditSuisse/Tremont Hedge Fund Index, 110–112
Crittenden, Eric, 72
Cross-market momentum, 159
Currencies, 115–116

D. E. Shaw hedge fund, 104
Dalio, Ray, 25, 166
DB Carry ETF, 116
DB Currency Returns Index, 116
Deflation, 62
Deutsche Bank, 115–116
Dexion Absolute, 122, 125–126
Dexion Alpha, 121
Dexion Equity Alternative, 128
Directional hedge funds, 100, 102–103
Discipline, 162–163, 185

Diversification, 22, 37, 50–53, 71,
  153, 159
Dividend funds, 119–120
Dogs of the Dow, 119
Dollar-weighted endowments.
  See Super Endowments
Domestic equity, 34–35
Dow Jones Industrial Average
  (DJIA), 119
Drawdowns, 59–60, 66, 135–136,
  137, 152

Easterling, Ed, 144
EDGAR database, 174
Efficiency, market. *See* Market
  efficiency
Efficient frontier, 23, 24
80/20 rule, 72
Einhorn, David, 95, 179–180
El-Erian, Mohamed, 49, 50, 51,
  53, 55, 66, 67–68, 70
Emerging stocks, 60–61
Emory University, 7
Emotions, 163
Endowment Management and
  Research Corporation
  (EM&R), 19–20
Endowments. *See also* Harvard
  endowment; Yale
  endowment
  asset allocation, 12, 13, 14
  differences from average
    investment portfolio, 4–8
  performance of, 11–14
  poor management of, 6–7
  returns, 12, 13, 14
  size of, 8–11

top 20 by size, 10
Equity:
  assets, 62
  domestic, 34–35
  foreign, 35–36
  funds, 88
  hedged, 116
  private (*See* Private equity)
ETFs (exchange traded funds), 47
  benefits of, 92–93
  private equity, 92–96
  sample Policy Portfolio, 75, 76
  using to build Policy Portfolio,
    55, 70
Extensions, 158–159
*Extraordinary Popular Delusions
  and the Madness of Crowds*
  (Mackay), 138

Fairholme Fund, 118
Fama French Factor model, 74
Fat tails, 148
Fees, 71, 105–106, 158–159,
  176, 191
Fisher, Philip, 139
Fixed-income funds, 37
*Fooling Some of the People
  All of the Time* (Einhorn),
  96, 179
Ford Foundation, The, 19, 65
Foreign equity, 35–36
Foreign listed hedge funds, 114,
  121–123, 129–130
Form 13F-HR. *See* 13Fs
Fraser-Sampson, Guy, 96
Fuller & Thaler Asset
  Management, 104

Fund of funds (FOFs), 92,
    103–112
    created by investor, 182–185
    drawbacks, 105–106
    largest, 123, 125–128
Futures, 70–71, 116–117, 176

Gains, 161–162
General partner (GP), 85
Gire, Paul, 167
Global Timber & Forestry Index
    Fund (WOOD) ETF, 47
Go anywhere funds, 117–118
Golden Circle, 83
Goldman Sachs Commodity
    Index (GSCI), 31, 154, 200
Goldman Sachs Dynamic
    Opportunities, 127
Goldstein, Philip, 173
Google, 83
Gottschalg, Oliver, 86
Graham, Benjamin, 176–177
Greenlight Capital, 179–180
Greenwich Alternative
    Investments, 111
Greer, Bob, 70
Griffin, John, 181
Grinnell College, 11
Gross, Bill, 50
GSCI. See Goldman Sachs
    Commodity Index (GSCI)

Harris Alternatives, 122
Harvard endowment, 3–4, 41–53
    annual returns, 42, 57, 58
    asset allocation, 50–53, 62,
        191–192

asset class performance, 52
history, 42–43
returns, 56, 63
structure compared with
    Yale's, 43
vs. S&P 500, 61
Harvard Management Company
    (HMC), 43–44, 48–50
Hedged equity, 116
Hedge Fund Research, Inc.
    (HFRI), 108, 111
Hedge funds, 49, 97–132, 189
    academic, 104–105
    assets vs. number of funds, 99
    benefits, 100
    bias, 107
    categories, 100
    drawbacks, 100, 101
    foreign listed, 114, 121–122,
        129–130
    individual, 123–125
    introduction to, 98–105
    largest, 123
    options to invest in, 112–123
    performance, 106–112
    portfolio development, 186
    practical considerations,
        131–132
    problems with tracking
        performance, 106–107
    strategies, 101–102
    and Super Endowments, 98–99
    U.S. listed, 115
    using indexes to track returns,
        107–110
    vs. 13F strategy, 175–176
    and Warren Buffett, 178

Heebner, Ken, 118
HEPI (Higher Education Price
    Index), 12, 29
Herding, 141
HFRI Fund of Fund Composite
    (HFRIFOF), 108
HFRI Weighted Composite
    Index (HFRIFWI), 108
Highfields Capital
    Management, 49
Holding period, 174–175
Holy Grail, 169
Hussman Strategic Growth
    Fund, 116

Ibbotson, Roger, 70, 95
Illiquid assets, 5, 37
Index funds, 71, 109
Indexing, 30–32, 71–74, 107–110
Inflation, 5, 6, 28–29, 62, 68–69
Information overload, 139
Initial public offering (IPO), 85
Internal rate of return (IRR),
    85, 91
International LPE Index, 95
Investment:
    horizon, 5
    return on, 64
    risk, 138
    volatility, 64
Investment Company Act of
    1940, 99
Ivy Portfolio, 62
    asset classes, 191–192
    building, 55–79
    drawdowns, 66
    implementing, 188–190

moving average timing model,
    156, 157, 203–204
rebalancing, 202–203
returns vs. Harvard and Yale
    endowments, 63
and risk-adjusted returns,
    64–65
sample using ETFs, 75, 76
vs. timing, 1972–2007, 155

Jacobson, Jonathan, 49
J-Curve, 85
Jones, Alfred Winslow, 97, 99
Journal of Financial Planning, 167
Just One Thing (Mauldin), 144

Kahneman, Daniel, 138–149
Kaplan, Paul, 95
Kindleberger, Charles, 138

Larson, Jeffrey, 49
Lehman Opta Private Equity
    (ETN), 95
Lending, securities, 44
Leverage, 97, 158–159
Leveraged buyout funds, 38
Limited liability companies
    (LLCs), 99
Limited partnerships (LP), 44, 85,
    90–91
Liquidity, 5, 175
Listed Private Equity (LPE)
    Index, 95
Litterman, Bob, 33
Little Book of Common Sense
    Investing, The (Bogle), 71
Logarithmic chart, 145

Long-term capital gains, 161–162

Long-Term Capital Management (LTCM), 105

Loss, 136–141, 161

Lowenstein, Roger, 105

Mackay, Charles, 139

Managed futures, 116–117

Management, active, 14–16, 31–32, 34–36

Man Group, 121

Manias, Panics, and Crashes (Kindleberger), 138

Margin fees, 158–159

Market efficiency, 33

Market timing, 140, 142, 144, 145–152

  and bear markets, 146–147

  and endowment returns, 166

  improvements, 158–159

  results 1973–2007, 152

Markowitz, Harry, 19, 22

MAR ratio, 66

Mauldin, John, 144

Mean reversion, 163–165

Mean-variance analysis, 22–24

Mendillo, Jane, 50

Merger arbitrage, 118

Merriam Capital, 162

Meyer, Jack, 41, 45–46, 48–50, 71

Mispricing, investment, 44

Momentum, 74, 115, 195–197

Monte Carlo simulation, 27

Moving average timing model, 140–142, 150, 151, 153–154, 156, 157

MSCI EAFE Index, 93, 153, 161, 200

Mutual fund, 115

NASDAQ, 93, 138, 142

National Council of Real Estate Investment Fiduciaries (NCREIF) Timberland Index, 46–47

Net asset value (NAV), 36

Nominal returns, 5

Nondirectional hedge funds, 100, 101

Nudge: Improving Decisions about Health, Wealth, and Happiness (Thaler), 104

O'Higgins, Michael, 119

Oil and gas assets, 38

Optimization, 148

Out of sample testing, 151–158

Overconfidence, 139

Passive Foreign Investment Companies (PFICs), 131

Paulson funds, 98, 121

Payout yield, 118

Pershing Square Capital Management, 121

PerTrac, 106

Phalippou, Ludovic, 88

Phaunos Timber Fund (PTF.L), 48

PIMCO, 50

Pioneering Portfolio Management (Swensen), 33, 38, 68, 77

Policy Portfolio, 13

construction based on Ivy
Portfolio allocation, 71
Harvard and Yale endowments
vs. S&P 500, 61
Harvard's, 44–46, 51
selecting, 188
using ETFs to build, 55
Yale's, 28–30, 33–34
Portfolio management, 175, 183,
187–193
Positive feedback loop, 90
PowerShares, 93
Princeton Newport Partners,
104–105
Private equity, 38, 44–45, 50,
83–96, 189
benchmarking, 85–92
ETFs in a portfolio, 94
how to invest in, 91–96
what it is, 84–85
Private Equity as an Asset Class
(Fraser-Sampson), 96
Private equity ETFs, 93–96
Prospect theory, 139
Putnam, George, 43–44

Quantitative system,
141–151, 167
Quantum Fund, 65
Quartile, 32

Real assets, 37–38, 62, 68–71
Real estate, 37, 56
Real returns, 5
Rebalancing, 77–78, 156, 157,
166, 191
Red Rocks Capital, 93

REITs (real estate investment
trusts), 56, 154, 201
Relative strength system, 159
Renaissance Technologies, 104,
106
Returns:
absolute, 39
excess, 140
expected, 25
Harvard and Yale endowments,
57
increasing, 158
nominal, 5
on publicly traded asset classes,
136–137
real, 5
risk-adjusted, 64–66, 142
Reversion, mean, 163–165
Risk, 30
exposure, 7, 117
management, 51, 53, 91,
140–141, 176, 189–190
reduction, 136, 140, 151, 190
Risk-adjusted returns, 64–66, 142
Robertson, Julian H., 180–181
Rotation funds, 119, 159–160, 166
Rule 10b–18, 120
Russell 3000, 72, 73
Rydex fund, 117

*Scenarios for Risk Management and
Global Investment Strategies*
(Ziemba), 65
Sector allocation, 114
Securities and Exchange
Commission (SEC), 173,
174–175

Securities lending, 44
Sequoia Fund, 177
Share repurchases, 120
Sharpe, William, 34
Sharpe Ratio, 17, 64, 65, 70, 91,
    159
Shaw, David, 104
Short sales, 176
Short-term capital losses, 161
Siegel, Jeremy, 141–142
Simons, James, 104
Simple Moving Average (SMA),
    141–142, 168, 169
Small cap market, 34
Smarter Investing in Any Economy
    (Carr), 74
Sortino ratio, 65
Sowood Capital, 49
S&P 500:
    average compounded growth
        rate, 177
    and Blue Ridge 13F clone, 182
    and Buffett 13F clone, 178–179
    below the 200-day SMA, 169
    compared with Harvard and
        Yale endowments, 3–4
    drawdowns 1984–2007, 60
    and Greenlight 13F clone, 180
    moving average timing model,
        142, 149, 150, 157
    performance, 59–60, 145, 147
    performance compared with
        equity funds, 88
    ten worst years *vs.* timing, 147
    total return 1973–2007, 199
    total returns *vs.* timing
        total, 144

vs. Policy Portfolios of Harvard
    and Yale endowments, 61
vs. 10-year government bonds,
    3-year rolling correlation, 26
yearly percentage returns *vs.*
    timing, 148
S&P Diversified Trend
    Indicator, 117
Sperandeo, Victor, 117
State Street Management, 43
Sterling ratio, 66
Stockcharts.com, 143
Stock replacement funds,
    117–118
Stocks:
    emerging, 60–61
    foreign developed, 60–61
    growth rate *vs.* Russell 3000, 73
    total returns, 1983–2007, 73
Stocks for the Long Run (Siegel),
    141–142
Stress test, 27
Subprime mortgages, 98
Super Endowments, 3–16
    active management of, 14–16
    advantages over smaller
        endowments, 15
    asset allocation, 12–13
    and hedge funds, 98–99
    returns, 59, 64
    size, 8–11
    as tool for selecting personal
        Policy Portfolio, 189
    vs. average endowments, 11
Survivor bias, 86, 95
Swensen, David, 17, 21–22, 33, 38,
    66, 67–68, 71–72, 77, 97

Systematic tactical asset allocation, 151–158

Tactical asset allocation, 140–141, 165–169
Taleb, Nassim, 72, 148
Tax-deferred accounts, 161
Taxes, 4–5, 95, 160–161, 176
Tax harvesting, 78, 189
T-bill yields, 167
TFS Market Neutral Fund, 116
Thaler, Richard, 104
Thames River funds, 121, 128
Third Point Offshore Ltd., 124
13Fs, 174–178, 183
Thomson Venture Economics, 85–86
Thorp, Ed, 104–105
3-year rolling correlation, 26
Tiger Funds, 180–181
Tiger Management, 65, 183
Timberland, 38, 46
Time-weighted returns, 85
Timing system. *See* Market timing
TIMOs (timberland investment management organizations), 46–47
TIPS (Treasury Inflation-Protected Securities), 61, 68
Trade distribution, 161
Trader Vic on Commodities (Sperandeo), 117
Transparency, 173, 175
Treasury Inflation-Protected Securities. *See* TIPS

(Treasury Inflation-Protected Securities)
Trend following, 195–197
Turnover, 161
Tversky, Amos, 138
Tweedy Brown funds, 177
2020 Vision (Liem), 25, 33, 166
Tykhe Capital, 121

Ulcer index, 66
Unconventional Success (Swensen), 66
University of Rochester, 6–7
U.S. listed funds, 115

Value, 116
Value-added investing, 38
Vanguard Windsor Fund, 65
Venture capital, 38, 44, 84, 89, 90
Venture Economics database, 89
VIX, 167
Volatility, 3, 35, 64
    clustering, 167
    expected, 25
    reduction, 152
von Bechtolsheim, Andreas, 83

Wash rule, 78
When Genius Failed (Lowenstein), 105
When Markets Collide (El-Erian), 49, 66
Wilcox, Cole, 72
Wilshire 5000 Index, 34–35
World Beta, 70

Yale endowment, 17–39
  annual returns, 57, 63
  annual returns *vs.* asset classes,
    58
  asset allocation, 21, 50, 62,
    191–194
  asset classes, 33
  contribution to operating
    budget, 8
  contribution to university
    revenue, 20–21
  expected returns and risk, 30

  historical private equity returns,
    90–91
  history, 18–21
  overview, 3–4
  private equity returns, 92
  returns correlated with Harvard
    endowment, 56
  vs. inflation, 6
  vs. S&P 500, 61
Yusko, Mark, 175

Ziemba, William T., 65

CPSIA information can be obtained at www.ICGtesting.com
Printed in the USA
BVOW03n2203180115

383345BV00006B/14/P